The Manifesto of Capitalism, 13th Edition

Capitalism: Adam Smith's Wealth of Nations,
Bible of Free Enterprise

with additional notes and an expanded preface

by
Frank Solomon

Light Brigade Publishing House

This book is dedicated to mankind who deserves a better economic fate than he has had in the past.

ALSO BY FRANK SOLOMON

The Manifesto of Capitalism, editions 1–12

The Gangster Papalardo, editions 1 and 2

Capitalism, editions 1-3

The Manifesto of Capitalism, 13th Edition

by Frank Solomon

ISBN 978-0-9991384-5-8

To hurt in any degree the interest of any order of citizens, for no other purpose but to promote that of some other, is evidently contrary to that justice and equality of treatment which the sovereign owes to all the different orders of his subjects,

(Adam Smith, *Wealth of Nations*, Bk. IV, ch. viii, p. 618)

If you want to understand how our investments are being despoiled and the nature of the criminals who are stealing our money, see Scorsese's *The Wolf of Wall Street.*

A movie reviewer opining on the radio

The *Wealth of Nations* I have referenced for this brief summary is the Modern Library Edwin Cannan edition put out by Random House from 1937 – 1975. If you are using another edition, the pagination will be different.

The *Manifesto of Capitalism 13th Edition* can be purchased as a soft cover from Amazon using ISBN 978-0-9991384-5-8. To purchase as a kindle from Amazon use ISBN 978-0-9991384-6-5.

Capitalism (2nd ed.) can be bought in soft cover or as an eBook from Archway Publishing.com; Log in Capitalism by Frank Solomon. eBook–ISBN:978-1-4808-0063-2; Soft Cover–ISBN:978-1-4808-0062-5. *Capitalism (2nd ed.)* may be purchased from Amazon using ISBN 978-1-4808-0062-5.

All Solomon's books can be purchased or downloaded from other major booksellers.

ALL THE DIRECT QUOTES FROM THE WORKS OF ADAM SMITH RETAIN THEIR ORIGINAL 18TH CENTURY SPELLING AND PUNCTUATION.

Table of Contents

PREFACE

Many well educated, intelligent people throughout the world are classical capitalists without realizing it, as they have not read *Wealth of Nations*, (1776), *The Theory of Moral Sentiments* (1759) or the other works of the father of classical capitalism, Adam Smith. Most economists familiar with Smith's *oeuvre* consider *The Theory of Moral Sentiments* and *Wealth of Nations* to be a single opus.

After reading the following list of prominent features that dominate Smith's economic system, many readers may realize they too are classical capitalists.

1) A scientific contemplation and adjustment to the ever-fluctuating facts and phenomena of life, especially those closely related to the economy. Education ought to be as universal as possible, since enlightenment fosters the comprehension of complex issues and liberty. (Evidence of God's existence is to be found in the harmony, beauty, and balance of nature). Balance in all things economic;

2) A reasonably strong identification with the nation. Strong, positive communal feelings and behavior necessary to the survival of the state and each citizen;

3) Approval of a pervasive attitude that each citizen should provide as best he can an adequate living for himself and his loved ones through an honest activity that helps other members of the community to survive in some way. (This helpful activity may be hauling, building, paving, nursing, defending, banking, sewing, entertaining, etc. Anything from bartending to brain surgery). The division of labor as the best method of creating the

greatest number of jobs, the most amount of wealth, and the firmest stability for any particular community; the wealthy should be required to contribute to the public treasury "somewhat more than in . . . proportion to their revenue". Minimum wage laws that would require an appropriate living wage to be the least any person could receive at a particular time and place; a net for the jobless most conducive to having them seek employment;

4) Fair competition, which would ban interference with supply and demand economics, except in calamitous situations;

5) Smith's 'laws of justice,' which comprise the following:

(a) Legislation eliminating all "unreasonable restraints of trade," such as force or violence of every sort;

(b) Legislation enforcing free and fair competition. The following would be banned: monopoly in most forms, price fixing, wage manipulation, bribery, theft, extortion, chicanery, fraud, etc.;

(c) Laws that would outlaw or not allow without proper regulation the practice or production of anything that might harm 'all of society.' For example, the sale of hardcore drugs to anyone, murder for hire, etc. would be banned. The pumping of poisonous industrial fumes into the atmosphere, the manufacture of all ordnance, et al. would be regulated;

As long as you follow the 'laws of justice', you can become as rich as Croesus without obstruction.

6) One is compelled to infer from these above enumerated restrictions, Smith powerfully asserts that over the long haul <u>HOW ONE MAKES MONEY</u> is more important to the salvation of the family, civilization, and the maintenance of just

order than how much money you make. Justice itself should be rendered expeditiously, with perfect fairness, and tend toward leniency in hope of the fullest rehabilitation. The pursuit of just and equal treatment for every member of society, regardless of race, creed, religion, class, gender or ethnicity;

7) Firmly backing trade agreements with other nations and the development of common markets – such as the European Union that presently exists – as ways to increase the wealth of each citizen and to diminish the chances of martial conflict; staunch opposition to any war not clearly defensive in nature. (The armed forces should be voluntary, made up of citizens who had picked soldiering as their trade); the support and promotion of democratic policies and structures, as these features protect free and full competition.

Smith did not embrace his friend Dr. Quesnay's physiocratic principle *laissez-faire, laissez-aller* (allow people to make and do what they please in the market-place). King Louis of France – Dr. Quesnay's patient –considered himself a citizen of the realm, albeit the wealthiest and most powerful citizen who sat on the throne of his realm by Divine Right. His decrees – which often followed the prescriptions of Dr. Quesnay – evinced his participation in the life of the nation. Louis did not regard his wise participation to be an instance of interference. Thus, his participation could not be interpreted in any way as a refutation of *Le monde va de lui-même*. The decrees of Louis were not laws – which would have inhibited the ruler – but proclamations. And they could be immediately rescinded – by King Louis himself. Smith reserves his admiration for Quesnay's work to the brilliance displayed in his friend's explanations and manipulations of economic theory.

Smith agreed no more with King Louis than with King George, and thus did not use the term *laissez-faire* in any of his writings, and even avoided it in his seventeen page discussion of physiocratic theory in *Wealth of Nations*. In the marketplace and everywhere else in society, people would have to be guided and limited by "the laws of justice", which came before all else in Smith's mind. After all, to a civilized man, fair laws were as natural as faith in a Supreme Being.

The Theory of Moral Sentiments examines how and why people identify with each other and how this process of identification is central to the creation of communal living. Compassion and reason are the main ingredients that allow people to cooperate. Compassion is instinctive and reflexive. Reason hones the direction, manner, and amount of moral sentiment expressed. Thusly conscience is made manifest.

Much as social animals in the wild live in packs or herds, which afford each creature an increased chance of an extended and healthy survival, so man creates communities that allow each member to enhance his or her opportunities for a prolonged and robust stay on this earth. A wolf who is not a lone wolf contributes to the survival of his pack, and his pack in turn provides him with a share of the kill and its protection from other predators. A human being contributes to his community with some form of industry that helps his culture to survive; in turn, his society provides him a living and a certain amount of protection from various dangers.

Laws and rules provide each society with its unique dimensions, shape, and identity. And although competition within a pack or community is inevitable and healthy, all rivalry must take place in an arena of strictures that preserves a culture's existence.

Wealth of Nations depicts how a free enterprise economy functions within a community that permits its introduction.

In every manner of serious literature, hundreds of references can be found to Smith and to his work in terms like the following: the Patron Saint of Capitalism; the father of classical capitalism; the sire of free enterprise; etc. P. J. O'Rourke calls Smith *"Capitalism's Champion," "Capitalism's Original Money Maven," and "Capitalism's Therapist,"* (P. J. O'Rourke, On the *Wealth of Nations,* New York: Grove Press, 2007), pp. 49, 52, 54. *Wealth of Nations* is often alluded to in scholarly works as the primary source of capitalism. A typical example taken from Thomas Fleming's *Liberty! The American Revolution* is as follows: "Adam Smith's *The Wealth of Nations*, the bible of capitalism, was published in 1776," (Thomas Fleming, *Liberty! The American Revolution*, New York: Viking Penguin, 1997. p. 42. Underlining mine). One of Smith's most highly regarded biographers observes, "Smith's championship of the 'obvious and simple system of natural liberty' in the economic sphere, historically has been interpreted as endorsement of a free enterprise, capitalist system," (Ian Simpson Ross, *The Life of Adam Smith*, New York: Oxford University Press, Inc., 1995), p. 417. In the introduction to the first Modern Library publication of the Edwin Cannan edition of *Wealth of Nations*, Max Lerner has written, "Adam Smith was, in his own day and his own way, something of a revolutionary. His doctrine revolutionized European society as surely as Marx's in a later epoch. He was on the economic side, the philosopher of the capitalist revolution, as John Locke was its philosopher on the political side," (Adam Smith, *Wealth of Nations*, New York: Random House, Inc., Modern Library edition, 1937) Intro. p. x. The McGraw-Hill *Encyclopedia of Economics*, 2nd edition, says: "This outline of the perfectly competitive capitalist economy was first popularized by Adam Smith," (John Cornwall, under "Capitalism," in The McGraw-Hill *Encyclopedia of Economics*, 2nd ed., New York, 1982), 133. As a final example the authoritative *Encyclopedia Britannica* states under capitalism, "The ideology of classical capitalism was expressed in Adam Smith's *Inquiry into the Nature and Causes of the Wealth of Nations* (1776)." Why should such weighty evaluations of Smith and *Wealth of Nations* be made by serious scholars in important reference works? Those people who judiciously seek an objective solution in a mixed economy will find that solution already judiciously mixed in Adam Smith's *Wealth of Nations*. A kind of time warp has taken place in regard to Smith's work. It is as though the author bearing the sobriquet Father of Classical Capitalism had boarded a time machine in the 18th century and flown ahead to the late 20th century. There Smith observed all the different politico-economic currents – some of which were flowing in opposite directions and creating whirlpools of violence. Nuclear war and the extinction of mankind were likely developments because of the inability of people to compromise. Then Smith returned home to the seventeen-hundreds and wrote a great synthesis of all the politico-economic systems he had observed circa 1975. This useful tome he called *Wealth of Nations*. It is the touchstone of the free enterprise system.

****

Smith is the great psychologist of the 18th Century. In his 1776 masterpiece he contrasts two forms of economic behavior. 'Mean rapacity' – the product of infantile selfishness – is juxtaposed with mature 'self-interest' that reflects a meaningful identification with other human beings. I state again, in his 1759 bestseller *The Theory of Moral Sentiments*, Smith details how and why people identify with one another and why this process plays a crucial role in the destiny of human beings.

As already noted, human beings are drawn together into productive communal living by compassion and reason, so it is not unreasonable to infer that the joy of helping others is the signature characteristic of a civilized man or woman.

Reasonable helpfulness eases all aspects of business and work. A businessman who naturally delights in aiding others is more likely to come up with a product, idea or service that is useful than someone who is indifferent to his fellow man, and he is more likely to hire people who are helpful to customers and fellow workers. When joined to intelligence and skill, the pleasure of assisting others is a trait which tends sharply to increase profits.

'Mean rapacity' inevitably ushers in a feverish jungle of severe economic decline. Mature 'self-interest' generally leads to economic growth with numberless happy advantages. Mature 'self-interest' is today called enlightened self-interest by professional economists, their preferred term for Smith's entire blueprint.

Smith's theory of 'enlightened self-interest' asks us to pay close attention to the facts and phenomena of human interaction in order to determine those patterns which are frequently repeated. This gives us a general understanding of human nature, which allows us to see that our own prosperity and survival depend upon the prosperity and survival of other people. Such a revelation leads to ethical practices. We can then further benefit ourselves and our community by using statistics and probability theory to predict future developments with increased accuracy – a result particularly useful in matters of business and policy.

When Smith urges self-interest in *Wealth of Nations* he is understood to be encouraging the economic endeavors of individuals who have developed some reasonable concern for their fellow man. 'Moral sentiments' were to be reinforced by laws which establish 'fair competition' and prohibit unreasonable restraints of fair trade. Smith's pivotal concept for the solution of economic problems is to release market forces to do most of the work. However, these market forces had to be guided by 'laws of justice' in order to benefit society. As previously noted, people could not be allowed to do whatever they wanted in the economic sphere.

His goal as a thinker was to give the public and legislators practical tools for the enrichment and stabilization of any realm. The mechanism of supply and demand is the author's main *tool* of analysis throughout *Wealth of Nations*. Smith's contemplation of such factors as the laws of supply and demand (Adam Smith, *Wealth of Nations*, Bk. I., ch. vii, pp. 55-63) led him to dilate on their effect on a variety of human institutions. Thus, he became known as a moralist, a reformer, and of course an abolitionist.* His philosophy as well implicitly extends itself to the right of women to be treated the equal of men in every regard.

As a result of his various analyses, Smith came to the conclusion that in economics how you made money was more important than how much money you made. Like most of the leaders of The Enlightenment, he reasoned that if the benefits of civilization were to be preserved and a just social order created, the problems of widespread poverty and starvation had to be solved.

*In The Theory of Moral Sentiments (1759) Smith caustically remarks: "There is not a Negro from the coast of Africa who does not … possess a degree of magnanimity which the soul of his sordid master is too often scarce capable of conceiving. Fortune never exerted more cruelly her empire over mankind, than when she subjected those nations of heroes to the refuse of the jails of Europe, to wretches who possess the virtues neither of the countries which they come from, nor of those which they go to, and whose levity, brutality, and baseness, so justly expose them to the contempt of the vanquished," (Adam Smith, *The Theory of Moral Sentiments*, Pt. v, ch. ii., pp, 206-207).

The extent to which poverty does not exist is one of the ways Smith judges the wealth of a nation. "It is the great multiplication of the productions of all the different arts, in consequence of the division of labour, which occasions, in a well-governed society, that universal opulence which extends itself to the lowest ranks of the people," (Adam Smith, *Wealth of Nations*, Bk. I., ch. i., p. 11). "Servants, labourers, and workmen of different kinds make up the far greater part of every political society. But what improves the circumstances of the greater part can never be regarded as an inconveniency to the whole. No society can surely be flourishing and happy, of which the far greater part of the members are poor and miserable. It is but equity, besides, that they who feed, cloath, and lodge the whole body of the people, should have such a share of the produce of their own labour as to be themselves tolerably well fed, cloathed and lodged," (Adam Smith, *Wealth of Nations,* Bk. I., ch. viii., pp. 78, 79. All emphasis mine.) Workers would be far more prosperous than they were, "had not the interested sophistry of merchants and manufacturers confounded the common sense of mankind" from its natural course, (Adam Smith, *Wealth of Nations*, Bk. IV., ch. iii, Pt. ii. p. 461.)

How do you make the distribution of wealth more equitable? And how does one convince the 2% – who commanded 98% of Britain's wealth – to go along with your ideas? A persuasively pragmatic plan had to be presented which demonstrated

"Avarice and injustice are always shortsighted," (Adam Smith, *Wealth of Nations*, Bk. III, ch. ii, p. 369.) Much of this plan would be based on what Smith calls the obvious fact that money was worth only what it could buy – especially in regard to life's necessities. The great majority of those 2% that owned 98% of England's wealth classified themselves as mercantilists who drew both cohesion and encouragement from Sir James Steuart's *An Inquiry into the Principles of Political Oeconomy* (1767). According to Smith, "Monopoly" was "… the sole engine of the mercantile system," (Adam Smith, *Wealth of Nations*, Bk. IV., ch. vii., Pt. iii, p. 595).

Smith set out, as one of his goals in *Wealth of Nations*, to explain to the well healed how they would grow even more prosperous were they to dispense with monopolistic practices. His argument also would help sustain the clamor for stern laws against monopoly that issued from the unwashed multitude. Legislatures would gather fresh reasons for interfering with the *status quo*. And anti-trust legislation would hold in check all practices deemed monopolistic – as part of an entire body of just laws Smith envisioned. No one would be able to reasonably object to the amount of wealth you could harvest so long as your riches were accumulated in accord with the laws of justice – fair competition – you paid each worker at least a living wage, you did not indulge in "unreasonable restraints of trade" such as brutality or violence of any kind, consistently did work of which you could be proud, and did no harm to the community or nation to which you owed allegiance.

Smith's attitude is famous in regard to private monopolies run by one or more individuals. Such monopolies were legal in England and totally unregulated. The largest monopoly ever created in the history of mankind was the African or British East India Company that Smith damns as incompetently run, unspeakably cruel, of benefit to only the richest men in England, and a means of beggaring the rest of the nation. As mentioned, Smith wanted laws that would destroy these barricades to economic justice. However, Smith did approve of several special kinds of monopoly, such as the following: 1) Public utilities run as permanent monopolies by cities, counties or the central government in regard to lighting and paving streets and other aspects of infrastructure. Why? Experience had shown that in Great Britain at least, private ownership in these matters swiftly led to bankruptcy or to vital work not being done. For private owners to break even, city streets went unlit and roads, bridges, canals, etc. went unrepaired. 2) (a) Temporary monopolies would be permitted in specific circumstances for people taking part in very dangerous projects such as exploring barbarous shores. If a temporary monopoly were not granted, these dangerous tasks would never be undertaken. (b) Temporary monopolies granted for a set number of years to authors and inventors through copyright. This was necessary in order to inspire ingenuity and to reward the efforts and the investments of capital, time, talent, and energy in creating various original works. Smith worked hard for the passage of meaningful copyright legislation, (Adam Smith, *Wealth of Nations*, Bk. V., ch. i., Pt. iii., Art. 1st, 2ndly, p. 712). 3) *Wealth of Nations* strongly suggests that all ordnance be manufactured by a single government owned monopoly. This would give considerable assurance that wars would not be initiated solely to generate profits for private investors in the arms industry. A discussion of these matters with detailed references to *Wealth of Nations* can be found in Frank Solomon's *Capitalism*, 2nd ed. (2013) Pt. One, Section II, pp. 72 - 73: (ISBN: 978-1-4808- 0062-2-5 sc).

By breaking up existing monopolies and preventing new monopolies from being formed, a maximum amount of rivalry would be created. Prices generally would fall as a result of burgeoning competition. These factors were already shaping the Industrial Revolution which economic historians tell us began circa 1760. (Adam Smith, *Wealth of Nations*, Bk. I, ch. i-ix, pp. 3-98); (Bk. II, Intro., ch. i-v, pp. 259-355); et al.

A mercantilist might complain that he would lose much of his net profit if monopolies were outlawed. The counter to this observation would be that with the obliteration of private monopolies and the establishment of a freely competitive market, prices might fall to such a level that the mercantilist who once paid 100 pounds of his old weekly net for his usual purchases would now spend only 50 pounds of his new weekly net for those same purchases. He probably would be wealthier than before because each pound sterling had increased so in value, he now needed many fewer of them to live as well as he had. A real calculation of his prosperity would depend upon how far his net profit had fallen in the same period.

However, as already indicated, the benefits of a sustained freely competitive market would be revealed by the following: an appreciable decline in poverty because competition would force prices to go down, while simultaneously increasing the number of job opportunities. Employers would tend to lure workers with the promise of higher salaries than they could earn elsewhere. Of course to avoid the gravest unrest, no worker could be paid less than a living wage proper for a particular time and place, as Smith asserts several times, (Bk.I, ch. viii, pp. 66-68, 74, 81); (Bk. V, ch. ii. Pt. ii, Art 4th, p. 824) et al. Thus the overwhelming majority of ordinary British subjects would be considerably better off under a free enterprise economy than under a mercantilist system.

Born into the Presbyterian faith, Smith evolved into a theist who believed that evidence of God's existence was everywhere in nature, and one could best comprehend the Supreme Being by scientifically contemplating the facts and phenomena of life. But he abhorred almost every aspect of organized religion.

Smith became a professor of logic at the University of Glasgow in 1751, and soon took over the instruction of moral philosophy as well. Naturally and necessarily, he was more than just familiar with both the *Old Testament* and the *New Testament*. His bestseller in 1759, *The Theory of Moral Sentiments*, is saturated with a notion of justice developed from passages in both Testaments and his ideas of what to do with our brief stay on earth are drawn from the words of God in *Genesis*.

Smith was obsessed with the concepts of justice and liberty. Perforce his main target in *Wealth of Nations* became the mercantilists who backed only unjust laws that preserved and fostered their riches. These mercantilists were the quintessence of 'mean rapacity,' the personification of criminality, and the embodiment of treason. Like Nazis, those finest examples of mercantilism we have to date, these creatures were willing to turn you and your loved ones into lampshades or lamb chops for one more pence or one more scintilla of power. In direct consequence of their behavior, profound poverty became common throughout the United Kingdom, leading to widespread disorder that imperiled the realm. Under conditions of havoc, any cohesive group can foist itself upon a host nation. In our own day, chaos may lead to domination by organized crime, drug cartels, Marxists or other totalitarians, OPEC, alien cultures, and enemy states. These aforementioned elements often make common cause to achieve their goals.

Smith's fixation on the interrelated notions of justice and liberty led him in *Wealth of Nations* to condemn the British Empire as exploitive, cruel, and impractical. He preferred a commonwealth or common market to an empire. Each country or region would have representation in parliament or the assembly of states in proportion to what it contributed to the general economy, (Adam Smith, *Wealth of Nations* Bk. IV., ch.vii., Pts. i, ii, iii, pp. 523-606). Necessarily, Smith also damned as peculiar to autocratic rule the many senseless wars engaged in by England, resulting in a wasteful effusion of British blood and British treasure. Only defensive conflicts were worthy of being fought.

On his many visits to Britain, Benjamin Franklin helped Smith do research for *Wealth of Nations*. Thomas Jefferson proclaimed Smith's masterpiece the best work he had ever read on political economy. Many of the Founding Fathers became familiar with Smith's *oeuvre.* Inevitably, *Wealth of Nations* became a major influence on the substance of *The Constitution of the United States.*

As a part of the laws of justice that Smith wanted to pass in order to create and maintain a freely competitive marketplace, he felt the need for laws to secure the state from the treasonous behavior of some businessmen: *But those exertions of the natural liberty of a few individuals, which might endanger the security of the whole society, are, and ought to be, restrained by the laws of all governments,* (Adam Smith, *Wealth of Nations*, Bk. II, ch. ii., p. 308.) Privately owned monopolies and all the handmaidens of these enterprises – senseless wars, assassination, arson, bribery, blackmail, violent threats and brutal actions of every sort – had to be *restrained by the laws of all governments*. In this regard, a few criminal 'exertions' that come to mind present in modern American society are as follows: the sale of powerful illicit drugs to minors; the willful maintenance of extreme poverty in many cities for the sake of profit or ideology; the sale of arms to violent criminals within the nation or to hostile foreign countries; by various means, encouragement of useless and senseless wars to swell the coffers of the military-industrial complex; manipulating markets for the enrichment of a few and the economic agony of entire continents; etc.

Each of the activities listed above would be anathema to any society that wanted to prosper and endure. With what label should we mark the people who attempt to enrich themselves by indulging in such activities? Anyone who knowingly aids and abets the activities of such beings becomes a danger to the state. Those people who consciously strive to engage in these activities for profit are traitors. Smith does advise us to seek our own self-interest for the best results; but he also strongly suggests that in seeking our own long term self-interest, we had best avoid taking any action that might injure our community or nation.

Bowden's *Killing Pablo*, about the criminal career of Pablo Escobar, informs us in April of 1986, President Reagan signed National Security Decision Directive 221, which for the first time declared drug trafficking a threat to national security. In America alone the number of hardcore drug addicts amounted to many millions. A large percentage of these addicts ranged between the ages 12–19. The number of teenagers addicted to narcotics has gradually risen since 1986, only partially because of a burgeoning population. For the reasons which follow, there is no action more treacherous than selling hardcore narcotics to minors.

Drugs such as heroin or crack cocaine form an immediate and powerful addiction that is nearly impossible to break. The first victims are will power, good judgment, objective observation, and the ability to function adequately at nearly any task without a sustaining dose of the addictive drug.

In 2017 alone, 72,000 Americans died because of overdosing on pain killers illegally bought from drug dealers (the same dealers who also sell opium, cocaine, crack, heroin, et al.) or made available by murderously avaricious pharmaceutical companies, administered legally as prescriptions from licensed physicians. How many died overdosing on heroin and crack-cocaine? What is the number of deaths in 2017 from the plagues of A.I.D.S., various liver diseases, blood disorders, embolisms, cancers, et al. directly related to narcotics addiction? Add to this figure the number of deaths in America in the same period from various misadventures, muggings, suicides, gunfights, gang violence, targeted assassinations, etc. traceable to the drug trade. Annually we spend hundreds of billions in inflated insurance rates for the extraordinary amount of damage done in inner city areas to people, privately owned dwellings, and stores, as well as publicly owned parks, buildings, facilities of various kinds, and equipment. We pay much greater amounts in taxes policing precincts of abysmal poverty, incarcerating people, providing medical care, and paying welfare benefits to the families of those who cannot work because of addiction.

The scourge of drug addiction has spread to middle-class and wealthy areas, to brokers, bankers, money managers, politicians, professors, doctors, and military men. Our ability to continue to exist as an independent society has been significantly damaged. The economy has been impacted profoundly; our skill at coming out on top in any kind of conflict is seriously jeopardized; the chances of an accidental nuclear exchange have ratcheted upward; the very survival of mankind increasingly dances on a razor's edge because of the problem of hardcore narcotics addiction.

Gangsters, racists, totalitarians of every stripe seek to increase the hellish poverty in which tens of millions of Americans live, so that they can expand the sale of illicit drugs, while degrading minorities and discrediting democracy and the free enterprise system. As deprivation swells, drug addiction expands, and this expansion accelerates the growth of poverty, burdening everyone who has a legitimate job with ever increasing taxes and insurance rates. The national economy is proportionately retarded. It is a form of treason to deliberately spread or deepen levels of poverty. The problem of drug addiction is aided and abetted by gun manufacturers and their lobbyists in Washington who continue to supply the underworld and other anti-social elements with weapons that only the police and the military should be able to obtain. The Second Amendment ought to be supported strictly within the severe limitations dictated by modern technology and the need to protect the safety of every citizen. In light of the many massacres of innocent school children in recent years, the following measures ought to be immediately adopted: 1) No civilian should be able to own a firearm more powerful than the Colt Forty-five carried by Wyatt Earp or have a hunting rifle more powerful than a Winchester '73. And these guns should all be signature weapons – firearms that only the registered owner can operate. 2) Bump stocks are now outlawed, but the penalties for passing on bump stocks – legally bought before the current legislation was passed –should be increased significantly. In addition, there should be a standing offer from every police department in America to buy back bump stocks and all assault weapons from owners for double the price these people originally paid. Furthermore, there <u>must</u> be a law preventing the creation of any computer generated three dimensional plastic weapon. (3) No one below the age of twenty-one should be able to purchase a gun, with the exception of properly authorized, active members of the military or police. 4) The most thorough background check must be given a civilian before he or she is able to purchase a gun of any sort. 5) And it would not be a bad idea to have at least one properly armed policeman in every school and place of worship when activities were under way.

Our Founding Fathers were dealing with a population that made part of its living from hunting and who needed to fight off hostile tribes. As well, they wanted every citizen to be prepared for a foreign invasion or be able to adequately fight back against a government that had grown tyrannical. It is difficult even to imagine they would have tolerated a situation in which citizens could commit mass murder on impulse. The present policy of the N.R.A. is to put the profits of gun manufacturers and gun salesmen first and the security needs of America second. Such avarice marks a special kind of treason.

By what name should we designate a person who helps start wars basically for the one purpose of making money, but perhaps has secondary goals in mind as well? One important secondary aim might be to distract the public gaze from intolerably unjust and illegal political practices. Why should the best of our citizens die or be wounded or driven mad so that the misdeeds of politicos, warmongers, and industrialists can be buried? Why should any innocent citizen be hurt because arms manufacturers and greedy officials want to feather their nests with taxpayer dollars? Does not such a process weaken our ability to defend the nation when we are forced to do so? Furthermore, could not a small conflict easily become a large war that might lead to a thermo-nuclear exchange spelling the end of mankind? Such shortsighted greed and lust for power constitute a crime more dark than treason, not only in regard to America, but in regard to the entire human race.

It is grotesquely subversive to conspire to rig markets for the enrichment of a few dozen swine and the economic impoverishment of billions, a situation that has led in the past to martial conflicts in which tens of millions have died, and today could lead to the end of our very own species. A term as damning as treason must be given such behavior.

If you want to show what a patriot you are, go after people involved in the treacherous activities enumerated above. Get together with other like-minded people. Seek proper training and join a group of citizens who are professionals at going after dangerous miscreants.

There are excellent reasons for leaving the little man alone. You are not diminishing criminality in America by sending Mr. Soanso to jail for selling two sticks of weed. You are adding to the trouble of widespread and major lawlessness. Why? When grave felonies such as the sale of hardcore drugs are being committed in front of your face, you are aiding and abetting the perpetrators of these crimes by diverting time, talent, energy, manpower, and money to an insignificant and counter-productive end. These last mentioned resources are always in short supply and must never be squandered. Furthermore, any individual who concentrates on minor transgressions is distracting the public from the real difficulties which beset our society. He or she might be trying to build a reputation on bullshit. In such circumstances, the more success a person registers in pursuit of relatively petty matters – even were they deemed felonies – the greater will have been his or her contribution to the long term destruction of the common good.

When the average citizen sees some nobody ruined for having done very little, while major crimes – such as hardcore narcotics dealing and its consequences – go uncorrected, he or she cannot help inferring the worst gangsters are in charge of the nation's destiny; and little people are being victimized to terrify the masses into silent submission. As a result, the democratic exchange of ideas is given a death blow. People feel anything they say about politics or economics or the mob can bring retribution of one kind or another, even if one is personally guilty of very little. You are a malcontent should you demonstrate 'a big mouth' and by the size of your oral cavity pose a danger to the realm. However, the self-appointed Guardians of the Universe – the idiot Benjy and his Klansman sidekick Billy Bob – never make clear what region of earth they are protecting. Are they securing the *Status Quo* of Corruption and Bigotry or the Township of Revanchist Communism or the County of Fascism or the Citadel of Fanatic Religious Beliefs or the Islands of Langerhans or Lilliput or Fairyland or some or all at once these sacred places?

To reiterate, a freely competitive marketplace cannot exist if people are afraid to speak their minds and be creative. The various criminal empires, drug cartels, totalitarians of every stripe, and every enemy state are given a leg up. Pettiness is encouraged. A small town mentality with its interminable inquisitions that spare only the children and the very old – to paraphrase F. Scott Fitzgerald – grips the republic. We are reduced to the inane chatter of our colorful primate relative, the mandrill ape, characterized by its relentless coughs and barks, a reflexive behavioral manifestation, to which his fellow apes reflexively reply.

La Cosa Nostra is truly the octopus of which Italians whisper, as are all the other crime syndicates like the Russian

Mafia that have lately come into existence. They seem to have a finger in every pie. Some mob bosses actually do own important legitimate enterprises outright and maintain a 51% interest in many others and have a large enough share of an imposing number of businesses to be quite influential. The most honest politician may be totally unaware he or she is being manipulated by the underworld because the corporations and individuals who ostensibly paid for an election campaign seem to be above board. Even careful researching will not uncover the name of a single individual connected to organized crime. Perhaps this is because important decision makers of record are sometimes only stand-ins for the actual owners. They are marionettes who obey any legal order given in exchange for an opulent lifestyle. If a puppet is foolish enough to cross his Masters, he quickly discovers his strings have been cut and he is in free fall.

Socialists would have us believe that money is the root of all evil. This is not true. It is the attitude of too many people toward money that is the root of all evil. How you make your money and what you do with your money are what count.

It is not sinful to be rich. Bill Gates remains one of the richest men in the world. But he made his tens of billions honestly, through his own genius and industry. His products have helped nearly everyone on earth, while helping to create the modern world. It is evident in everything he has done that he enjoys aiding other people. The former mayor of New York, Michael Bloomberg, has made his billions through ingenuity and hard work. He too has demonstrated in a dozen pragmatic ways a desire to help other people. John F. Kennedy – a very rich man in his own right – through his brilliance and dedication assisted many disenfranchised and persecuted Americans, which was his joy as well as his legacy. John McCain, only moderately well off, strove for years to get Big Money out of our politics. Smith says in this regard, "But the mean rapacity, the monopolizing spirit of merchants and manufacturers, who neither are, nor ought to be, the rulers of mankind, though it cannot perhaps be corrected, may very easily be prevented from disturbing the tranquility of any body but themselves," (Adam Smith, *Wealth of Nations*. Bk. IV., ch. iii, Part ii, p. 460.) President Obama, a man of modest means, seems to have swallowed lock, stock, and barrel all Smith's works, which has shown favorably in both his magnificent rhetoric and most of what he tried to accomplish while in office. Obama helped America to revive economically. Each of these men – along with many other unnamed figures – represents classical capitalism and Adam Smith would have approved of each of them as among the finest exemplars of his politico-economic philosophy.

However, Smith asserts that anyone who stays within the laws of justice while strictly seeking his own gain – will help his society without any intention of doing so.

Unfortunately, there are many people – often extremely wealthy people – who possess in abundance and quite profoundly all the moral rectitude of Al Capone, the *weltanschauung* of Attila the Hun, and the business ethics of Pablo Escobar. Naturally, in accord with these models, they make up the most hideous gang of poisonous little worms the Lord ever tolerated to slither across the surface of this planet. Only for self-protection or material gain would they ever help another living creature beyond their extended families. They are not capitalists in Smithian terms.

The aforementioned creatures described so harshly are precisely the miscreants against whom Adam Smith fought. Smith called them mercantilists. They are known today as oligarchs. Our modern American oligarchs see eye-to-eye, in most respects, with the oligarchs who have taken over Russia. Why? Everyone of them on both sides believes in monopoly. As monopolists, they control most of the wealth in their respective nations, and they behave like 18th century European nobility.

Most of the occupations and wages of the common people issue from the largesse of the oligarchs. In Russia their hold on the state is reinforced and magnified by an oligarchical political system presided over by a Czar. In America we have a *de facto* oligarchical political system.

Big Money controls our politics on every level, but the opulent deliberately maintain an illusion of democracy to dupe the common man. People vote, but their votes mean nothing. Elected officials have to please the rich corporations and individuals who paid for their election campaigns.

Some of our American oligarchs are quite susceptible to blackmail or bribery by Moscow because their investments in Russia are much greater than Russian investments in the U.S. Our oligarchs cannot put the same squeeze on the Russians as the Russians can put on them. And Russia is a closed society. People who know they are being watched tend to be much more careful than people who assume they are not being watched. It is also more difficult to get accurate information second-hand on citizens of a totalitarian state. Additionally, the Kremlin would quickly eliminate any citizen who found himself or herself in a hopelessly compromised situation.

Despite the above facts, before the Covid-19 pandemic hit the human race, our economy appeared healthier than a short time before. This is because Washington belatedly confronted enterprises, which had fled abroad, with legislation designed to see their net profit from their establishments in foreign lands would amount to less than had those same businesses been left at home. Consequently, many businesses have come back; and very few have chanced leaving. (We must hope any fresh tax break favoring the rich will be accompanied by warnings that if they do not invest their additional wealth in the U.S. – to create more jobs and greater wealth for the lower and middle classes – the I.R.S. will be instructed to examine their books with infinite care). These measures seem both wise and necessary. But at best they are just temporary. Only the future will reveal if any new tax break helps us.

To curtail the power of hostile states over our fate, we must purge Big Money from our politics. Federal, state, and local elections must be funded by treasury funds only. No private backing can be tolerated. And we must revive our anti-trust laws and add to them more potent anti-trust legislation. The above tactics might eventually shrink the power of the oligarchs, both domestic and foreign.

The tiger is in charge of the cattle pens. Let us go forward together, shoulder to shoulder, and drive back this monster to the dark forests whence he came. Let us prevent the future from becoming an endless torment of unrest, a future where we would suffer the drumbeat of endless wars. We must avoid such an awful destiny that would make us the playthings of alien natures, the clay of alien dreams.

Our logo is the abstract of a thriving mall encircled by the following capitalist motto: "Justice for all through fair competition." The term friend can serve capitalists the same function as the word 'comrade' does for communists; and the upraised thumb above a closed fist that pilots give on takeoff can serve capitalists as a salutation. Blue has always stood for liberty. Let the color blue symbolize the spirit of classical free enterprise.

Part I

From the day Adam Smith's *Wealth of Nations* went on sale in Britain, March 9th 1776, Smith's mercantilist enemy – who enjoyed for its own profit nearly total freedom to wreck the economy of the United Kingdom and the British Empire – sought to suppress Smith's economic principles. Mercantilism in the 18th century was supported in its endeavors by English law that explicitly backed unregulated monopoly, price fixing, scurrilous wage manipulation, and various forms of bribery.

Mercantilists have fought tooth and nail Adam Smith's laws of justice. Upon establishment of his system, "Every man, **as long as he does not violate the laws of justice,** is left perfectly free to pursue his own interest his own way, and to bring both his industry and his capital into competition with those of any other man or order of men," (Adam Smith, *Wealth of Nations*, Bk. IV., ch. ix., p. 651). Following this statement in the same paragraph, Smith writes that one of the obligations of a sovereign or chief executive *would be the duty of protecting, as far as possible, every member of the society from the injustice* and oppression of every other member of it, or the duty of establishing an exact administration of justice, (Ibid.). *Wealth of Nations* from first word to last, concerns itself with economic behavior. Thus, a reader is compelled to infer "the duty of protecting every citizen from injustice and oppression or establishing an exact administration of justice" must encompass fashioning 'laws of justice' to regulate the marketplace in favor of fair competition and the natural flow of trade.

These aims would be accomplished by outlawing any form of unnecessary interference with a level playing field, which would include that type of interference posed by most forms of monopoly, price fixing, wage manipulation, and bribery. "Commerce, which ought naturally to be, among nations, as among individuals, a bond of union and friendship, has become the most fertile source of discord and animosity," (Adam Smith, *Wealth of Nations*, Bk. IV., ch. iii., Pt. ii, p. 460.) Smith tags the underlying causes "of discord and animosity" as unreasonable restraints of fair commerce:

> Those mutual **restraints** have put an end to almost all fair commerce between the two nations. The principles that I have been examining in the foregoing chapter took their origin from private interest and the spirit of monopoly: those that I am going to examine in this, from national prejudice and animosity. They are, accordingly, as might well be expected, still more **unreasonable**., (Adam Smith, *Wealth of Nations*, Bk. IV, ch. iii, pt.1, p. 441. Emphasis mine.).

Any philosophic text can give only a few concrete examples of abstract concepts. These few examples point to the much larger package of examples the philosopher invites his reader to discover outside his book.

In the two long chapters he specifically devotes to unreasonable restraints of trade and in some other parts of *Wealth of Nations*, Smith gives several examples which must be dealt with because they interfere with fair commerce and its natural flow. The ones of greatest importance are as follows: legal statutes that interfere intentionally or coincidentally with fair competition, creating the constrictive practices listed earlier, as well as many unnecessary tariffs, port duties, and bounties; the restriction by closed-shop regulations in favor of a few workers from the great pool of many who could be otherwise employed for a living wage in a particular trade or industry; rioting; bullying; threats of violence; physical coercion of any sort; conspiracies that significantly effect the economy, which would include fraud, theft, war for the sake of profit, piracy, slavery and less obvious types of exploitation of any class of people at home or among native populations abroad. A few of the activities exercised for profit which demonstrate unreasonable restraints of trade not specifically discussed in Smith's treatise are as follows: insider trading and stock rigging, rape, blackmail, pillage, kidnapping, arson, etc.

A perceptive reader should infer the ensuing from a perusal of Smith's text: Anything should be eliminated that threatens to unnecessarily disrupt or obstruct the even playing field of fair commerce provided by political freedom. This interference may be direct or indirect. It may fall into any one of the following categories: psychological assaults of various kinds; physical assaults of one sort or another; legal assaults embodied in statutes which create economic injustice; conspiracies of every sort; etc.

The interference alluded to above may be aimed at or effect any one or all or any combination of the following: some rival(s) or potential rival(s); customers, potential customers or consumers across-the-board; a specific class or classes of taxpayers, all taxpayers or people in the general population.

When the activities of any individual(s) in the marketplace might also endanger the security of the whole society, government is justified in interfering with these practices: "But those exertions of the natural liberty of a few individuals, which might endanger the security of the whole society, are, and ought to be, restrained by the laws of all governments," (Adam Smith, *Wealth of Nations*, Bk. II., ch. ii., p. 308). A few exertions that come to mind are as follows: the sale of powerful addictive narcotics to minors; the willful maintenance of levels of abysmal poverty in many areas for the sake of profit or ideology; the sale of tobacco products to the general public without proper cautionary warnings; the unregulated and widespread emission into the air of chemicals harmful to life; the sale of dangerously defective machines to the general public; the sale of arms to violent entities within the society or to hostile foreign states; the incitement to engage in useless martial conflicts to increase one's wealth; rigging markets for the benefit of a few and the impoverishment of many; et al. There is not one of these 'exertions' that would not also adversely effect immediately or eventually the conditions of fair competition and the natural flow of trade.

For the great multitude of human beings, the normal laws of justice which activate, preserve, and encourage fair competition in the marketplace evolve naturally from man's social instincts and simultaneously appear in harmony with the civilized desire to barter and exchange. At first these strictures will appear as tacit agreements, several of which may be articulated explicitly with the passage of time. Smith observes that sometimes this natural evolution of one culture or another toward just competition in economic matters is interfered with by political or historical events that force upon the marketplace some form of feudalism or mercantilism which largely excludes competition of any sort.

And although feudalism or mercantilism may persist in one society or another for hundreds of years, it is usually not permanent. This civilized desire to barter and exchange that might develop in a particular people, issues from and facilitates the deepest instinctive tendency of each person to preserve his or her own life. At this turning point, the ferocity of a savage – that seems to maximize each person's chances of survival in a loosely organized troop of hunters – combines with the social instincts of the bee latent in all of us. Each individual no longer must be a jack-of-all trades in order to survive, but is able to concentrate his attention on one occupation at which he excels: as a butcher, hunter, fisherman, arrow-maker, farmer, baker, et al. The instinct of self-preservation in harmony with group needs is reflected upon as sensible after it proves itself in pragmatic terms, and reason then hones the efficiency and effectiveness of this marriage. In the most recent speculations by anthropologists concerning Smith's description of the division of labor, if seasonal gardening were to become farming, necessarily the group's habitat must have become fixed for one reason or another in a single location instead of shifting with the seasons. This prolonged stay was probably meant to be temporary. But with the discovery of a more efficient and effective way of adequately feeding the entire extended family, its nomadic existence would come to a close. This sort of development tended to accelerate the division of labor. It is demonstrably true that a baker does not enter his trade for the good of the community, but out of self-interest. He notices there is a demand for bread, so by supplying this need is likely to receive for himself and his dependents at least an adequate living and perhaps even prosper. So he becomes an integral member of a community of families that comes to depend upon him for one important element in its routine diet. At the same time, his family comes to depend upon the community for all its daily needs other than baked goods.

Self-interest also guides this same person away from becoming a highwayman who might prosper greatly. For his riches, the highwayman would give nothing to those he robbed, but grief and diminished wealth. His crimes make him a hated outlaw that would be hanged on the spot were he caught. As a baker, if observed putting his thumb on the scale, he might be reproved by an angry patron, to whom he could offer some excuse. In order not to lose customers, he probably amends his behavior. There would be no chance of losing his life or his livelihood or ending up in prison. The fear of dire punishment inhibited most men of Smith's day from becoming bandits, as it inhibits most people today from robbing banks. The reflexive nature of self-preservation in the average person nearly always includes weighing consequences. Thus, enlightened self-interest begins its life as common practice.

In accord with most other intellectuals in what has come to be designated The Age of Reason, Smith at least gave lip service to the idea that man was both good and reasonable. But among men were those aberrant individuals who practiced 'mean rapacity' and sought to interfere with the natural harmony of 'free commerce'. These people managed to abuse the marketplace to such a degree that it became a vast jungle worthy of the kind of description rendered by Thomas Hobbes in *Leviathan*.

However, the social behavior of good and rational people like Adam Smith himself would eventually assert itself and correct society. What would society look like if fair competition were allowed to saturate the marketplace? From the perspective of an 18th century reader, the contours of Smith's futuristic view were intriguing. For example, in speaking of the high tariffs placed upon imports that competed with domestic manufactures, Smith points out that many foreign imports, some of superior quality to those produced in England, could sell at competitive prices in Britain, were the tariffs on these foreign goods repealed.

High tariffs forced most people to buy the domestically made item, creating a near monopoly of the home market for English businessmen. And of course each foreign country placed high tariffs on imports of goods from the United Kingdom in competition with those produced at home. Thus you got "a balance of trade" that Smith ridicules. Per force, Smith introduces the idea of a common market. The implementation of a system "of free exportation and free importation" would bring about the breakup of many domestic monopolies and some businesses might have to down-size or close entirely. The average businessman's nominal net might be less than before, but he might also end up with the same or a better standard of living, as his overhead and cost of living would be lower. But if a small number had to lower their standard of living somewhat, a comfortable income could still be maintained. Very few would be forced out of business. If some citizens went bankrupt, the same skills they had honed in one business would likely be useful in another and some of the same machines used in one business could be adapted for use in some other lines of work. But changes that would have such an effect should "never be introduced suddenly, but slowly, gradually, and after a very long warning," (Adam Smith, *Wealth of Nations*, Bk. IV., ch. ii., p. 438). This would allow owners and employees time to adjust to the new situation. The owner would have time to retool, diversify, etc. (Ibid.) The workers could be let go a few at a time over a long period instead of all at once, (Ibid., pp. 435, 436). Flexibility of this sort is common and natural. It is man's ability to adapt that has led to his survival.

If prices were to decline across-the-board and wages tend to remain the same, the average worker would grow much wealthier. At some point of course were prices to importantly rise above what an average worker could afford, families would starve. It is for this reason that Smith suggests a living wage as a minimum wage established by law that would make it adjustable to any rise in the price of necessities, (Adam Smith, *Wealth of Nations*, Bk. V, ch. ii., Pt. ii., Art. 4th, p. 824). Smith was interested in the wealth of nations – of workers, servants, and poor tradesmen *en masse* in a country or group of countries. Reliable averages and statistics would reveal what it took in income to keep an individual alive and healthy. He was not interested in fostering the wealth of rip-off artists. *Had not the interested sophistry of merchants and manufacturers confounded the common sense of mankind* from its natural course, the average citizen would tend to be more prosperous than he now was, (Adam Smith, *Wealth of Nations*, Bk. IV., ch., iii., Pt. i, p. 461).

For the species to survive, the essential goodness and reason of man must prevail over 'mean rapacity'. Man – the synthesis of all men taken together – will tend to convert a deadly swamp into a pleasant meadow – through the creation and application of laws of justice. But these statutes created by society must be contemplated by each citizen as a part of the **natural state** of civilized man in order to most effectively adjust, for his own purposes, his personal goals and his means to those real opportunities within his grasp: *Every individual is continually exerting himself to find out the most advantageous employment for whatever capital he can command. It is his own advantage, indeed, and not that of the society, which he has in view.* ***But the study of his own advantage naturally, or rather necessarily leads him to prefer that employment which is most advantageous to the society,*** (Ibid., ch. ii, p. 421. Emphasis mine) Thus – in Smith's view – given a choice between buying a seat on the stock exchange to become a stockbroker who could make money without regard for the consequences of his actions or spending his money for medical school to become a doctor who might mend people, a man of average character – being endowed with goodness and reason, as well as scientific and financial skills – would naturally and necessarily choose the healer's path. He would think in terms of the dignities that might be bestowed on him and the reverence and affection in which he might be held by those whom he helped. At the same time, he would shrink from the suspicion and dislike that might fall upon him as a broker. These thoughts would be reinforced naturally by a soothing sensation, accompanying the expression of his compassion each imagined cure would bring. And although he might over time average less money as a doctor than as a financial manipulator, he would have excellent prospects of accruing enough wealth to keep any sane man happy, while maintaining a more stable income year to year. Ergo, within the limits of those talents he possessed, what would most benefit him in the long run would become identical with what would most benefit society in the long run. Only that rare deviant would choose the perverse path of 'mean rapacity.'

****

Smith created classical capitalism itself – with its laws of justice – which eventually led to the introduction of fair play and free commerce into the agora. Necessarily, his politico-economic stance also led to the amendment or repeal of many laws that had aided and abetted unreasonable restraints of trade. "Commerce, which ought naturally to be, among nations, as among individuals, a bond of union and friendship, has become the most fertile source of discord and animosity," (Ibid., ch. iii., Pt. II., p.460). Of course, Smith did not have to address the infusion of billions into the finances of England from sources in bed with Isis. Nor could he foresee the tremendous influence of organized crime in all its manifestations, whose most powerful members were loyal to certain primitive cultural forms rooted in the 12th century.

Part II

To help bring 'scholarship' into concord with common sense, a useful dictionary ought to denote as **primary:** a capitalist is one who believes in the politico-economic philosophy of capitalism; i.e., an exponent of Smith's principles in *Wealth of Nations*. This reference book should state as well that all other usages of the term are **secondary**, the result of common parlance, for example designating someone a capitalist simply because that person was rich or made investments.

Mercantilist opposition to Smith's ideas in reality has always been a criminal conspiracy. It has no compunction about tipping its hat to what we now refer to as Orwellian language by defining terms according to a flagrant distortion of their primary meanings. And this quasi-Orwellian vocabulary was forced upon all reference books available to the general public, such as *Webster's International Dictionary,* the most popular lexicon available several decades ago. Thus – in accord with what mercantilist diction demanded – this influential source defined the word 'capitalist' as "One who has capital; one who has capital for investment or has capital invested." These denotations taken together included just about everyone on the face of the earth. If you were a pauper in Hong Kong and had the equivalent of a half pence in your jeans, you were technically a capitalist. Concern was generated among some thoughtful people who had other interests in mind.

But the stated definitions were insisted upon, despite the analyses of a consensus of leading etymologists that primarily a capitalist was anyone who backed Smith's free enterprise design in economics. Under pressure, the standard dictionary definition gradually changed, so that it became "1. a person who has capital, especially extensive capital, invested in business enterprises" or "2. an advocate of capitalism" or "3. a very wealthy individual". However, when a person used the word, an interested listener might be inclined to ask how the term was meant. Confusion was generated in the ordinary citizen. Finally, in its most up-to-date form, with the intention of pleasing every rich individual no doubt, the three aforementioned meanings of the word have been conflated into approximately the following: "a wealthy person who uses money to invest in trade and industry for profit in accordance with the principles of capitalism." Let us unpack this most current definition.

Firstly, the adjective *wealthy* is a relative term. A man with a minimum wage job who is just scraping by is wealthy compared to the vagrant that has no job, no means of support such as a welfare stipend, and lives under a bridge. Secondly, most people who are gainfully employed in even the lowest paying occupation have either a checking account, savings account or both. All normal savings accounts pay interest, and most checking accounts pay some interest also. If our minimum wage earner has any interest bearing account, **were** it **to pay no more than a penny a year**, he would be using his "money to invest in trade and industry for profit." He is making use of the banking industry, which takes its customers' deposits to invest in a variety of businesses that of course includes trades of different sorts. Lastly, there are nearly as many different sets of "the principles of capitalism" as there are people interested in economics. But very few of these people are engrossed in a scholarly investigation of free enterprise principles.

Some of the people currently involved in industry or business would say that the principles of capitalism are embodied in Adam Smith's opus. Those that did, probably would not say so because they had read *Wealth of Nations* and had formed an independent judgment. Their assertion would issue from hearsay or something remembered from one of their courses on economics. And their private reflections on capitalism almost certainly would include **the entirely false notion** that Adam Smith was *laissez-faire*. Smith never used the term in any of his works and disapproved of a good part of Quesnay's theory, which he analyzes through seventeen pages in his great tome. Without fanfare or much success, since the book's appearance, many researchers have noted that Smith was not a believer in the *laissez-faire* economic philosophy. One of the most prominent Adam Smith biographers has written: "… *laissez-faire* [is] a phrase which [Smith], never personally used, and is more appropriately associated with Quesnay and the Physiocrats," (Ian Simpson Ross, *The Life of Adam Smith,* New York: Oxford University Press, Inc., 1995, p. 275). Ross references five well-known contemporary sources to back up his assertion, among them Andrew Stewart Skinner, an esteemed Adam Smith scholar at Glasgow University.

The investor who is marked a capitalist in the public's mind because he has appeared in the newspapers as a major stockholder, may in fact be anything but an adherent of Smith's politico-economic philosophy. Many businessmen who regularly carry out immense frauds, and who can only be characterized as driven by pathological greed, call themselves capitalists. So a good part of the general public has developed an intense hatred for these specimens and cringe at the very word capitalist. The general public believes capitalists to be no better than murderous thugs. These businessmen – among which one may find several narcotics kingpins – have such tremendous and broad holdings, they have successfully helped to suppress the truth about what Adam Smith actually wrote, thought, and stood for. Per example, I have yet to find a book jacket of any edition of

Wealth of Nations that does not say or strongly suggest that the text supports *laissez-faire* economics and that Smith said or wrote that the marketplace should be left strictly alone.

After being hit by these bold-faced lies, it is only the book itself the potential reader leaves strictly alone. Smith never comes close to giving such foolish advice. But scholars and intellectuals have very little money and few means to combat such deliberately channeled poison. Additionally, many popular "reference works" – as notoriously misleading as Wikipedia – are published by owners who choose to pull the wool over the public's eyes. And a stick or carrot of one sort or another is usually at the ready to convince most scholars to get into line.

In addition Smith never says you have to have a penny or investments of any kind to be a true follower of his philosophy. Even a penniless hobo might become an advocate of free enterprise. And there would be some with investments who became exponents of Smith and some without investments who became exponents of Smith.

Under capitalism, *The Encyclopedia Britannica* says, "The ideology of classical capitalism was expressed in Adam Smith's *Inquiry into the Nature and Causes of the Wealth of Nations* (1776)." Occasionally responsible people are able to get Smith's message out. Circa 1890 the term "free enterprise" first appeared in print. It is a synonym for the expression "free commerce" used by Smith in *Wealth of Nations* and means exactly the same thing. *The Random House Unabridged Dictionary* tells us that it is "an economic and political doctrine holding that a capitalist economy can regulate itself in a freely competitive market through the relationship of supply and demand with a minimum of governmental intervention and regulation." This is a superb encapsulation of Smith's economic philosophy.

Smith felt that interference should only be made when it was necessary to preserve fair competition and the free flow of trade or to regulate a product, practice or situation that endangered "the security of the whole society." Etymological study, grammatical structure, and logic demand firstly a capitalist be defined as someone who is an exponent of Smith's politico-economic philosophy. However, it is always easier for exploiters to lead around by the nose citizens who are thoroughly bewildered, so premeditated obfuscation goes on apace.

Among the streams of thought found in *Wealth of Nations*, one prominent theme that dominates Smith's text is the idea that reason and humanity should always guide the behavior of people in charge. Smith was an abolitionist, and the word 'masters' in the following quotation was used in the England of Smith's time the way we use the term 'bosses' in America today. It was not intended to intimate mastery over slaves: *If masters would always listen to the dictates of reason and humanity, they have frequently occasion rather to moderate than to animate the application of many of their workmen*, (Adam Smith, *Wealth of Nations,* BK. I, ch. viii., p. 82). This would be a measure taken to increase net profits, as the health of workers is intimately tied to their productivity. It is a tactic of enlightened self-interest.

Enlightened self-interest is indeed the label most often used by scholars to designate Smith's politico-economic scheme. Smith's system is meant to be a transcendent doctrine, containing transcendent values and structures relevant to all activity that might effect the economy. Economic and social stability is the pivotal value being offered. The system aims at the stabilization of society through preservation of the conditions of fair competition that allows business and industry to flourish.

As noted, Smith's system depicts the synthesis of political liberty with a marketplace that seeks to sustain over time the greatest amount of competitive freedom. As economics affects all aspects of life and is effected in turn by every aspect of life, Smith delves into many areas of human behavior at first glance not directly related to economics, such as religious activity, education, philosophical speculation, scientific development, political debate, et al. He depicts how each area of human endeavor is related to and influences every other area of human endeavor, creating an ever-fluctuating variety of products and lifestyles along the way. Thus, Smith's work represents a morphology of human development as it pivots around economics. The insight necessary to create this morphological study known as *Wealth of Nations* has proven its value over the centuries. Smith's various formulations enhanced greatly the ability of businessmen and legislatures to predict how the economic sphere would react under a given set of real or hypothetical circumstances. **This is especially true in regard to his synthesis – from many different sources – of what is commonly referred to as the laws of supply and demand found in Book I, chapter vii of his masterpiece.** Apparently, Smith did for economics what Newton had done for physics. He invented it – for all practical purposes.

Democracy with its sensible flexibility provides to every service, item, and idea the necessary protection from interference in the marketplace. Democracy must be counted as much a part of classical capitalism as the urge to compete itself. Therefore, political freedom is a precept that must be guarded by particular institutions and given special legislative protections and powers not provided any other notion. In a free enterprise economy, liberty is to all other ideas what banking is to all other industries.

The banking industry – unlike any other industry, except energy – also must have unique protections and powers and follow special rules set by farsighted individuals and established institutions. The central role of the Federal Reserve Bank is the fostering of economic stability. Thus, it is given the power to regulate interest rates for loans; it is the financial institutions in the modern world that provide individuals and businesses what they need to prosper so that the economy can grow.

Everyone desires to be able to chart the expression of his or her own sexuality, lifestyle, aesthetic tastes, political concepts, philosophical ideas, and religious proclivities. The question for each of us is, "How do I protect my right to make these decisions and to maintain the choices I have made and to defend whatever new paths I might desire to take?" In order to protect over time one's own freedom to choose, one must protect the freedom of everyone in society to choose. An answer that adequately satisfies such concerns can best be found in an understanding and commitment to Smith's system. Why?

Under free enterprise, **discretion and good judgment** are the watchwords. Smith wants to use liberty as a tool to see that fair commerce becomes a sustained reality. His goal is the creation and preservation of evenhanded competition throughout the marketplace for the benefit of every member of society. He does not value – like some inebriated teen – freedom for the sake of freedom. He does not favor liberal doctrines so that flimflam artists dangerous to the very existence of the nation can wave a sophisticated flag to justify their avarice or any grotesque expression of their greed.

When interference begins to take shape in the marketplace, it is fair rivalry that must be our first concern, not some ideal of absolute political freedom. Competition must triumph over confrontation. Each citizen must be willing to make reasonable concessions. Leaders and businessmen in a capitalist society must exercise **discretion and good judgment** so that violence can be avoided and the valuable muscle of democracy not wasted. Otherwise political freedom itself will rapidly vanish. The concepts of Hugh Hefner must be able to compete fairly with the ideas of the Dalai Lama. Civilized debate between all parties should be welcome because such orderly dialogue tends to stimulate the sale of ideas through every outlet. But proponents of free enterprise do not want the adherents of Hefner's Playboy Philosophy to fall into physical altercation with the adherents of Tibetan Buddhism. Such combat would disrupt the essential rhythm of the marketplace.

In addition, only a marketplace that embraces political freedom can see to it that every aspect of the financial world is open to the examination, guidance, and regulation which might be necessary for it to remain over time as freely competitive as possible. Then enlightened self-interest can be sustained to keep in place mechanisms that forestall the intrigues of the military-industrial complex, insider traders, hostile foreign entities, the conspiracies of Fat Cats to rig the stock market, et al. This inspection and power to balance must exist in order to keep prolonged or repeated economic mayhem from encompassing society.

Economic chaos tends to destroy every important feature of freedom. When political freedom disappears, you can kiss goodbye your ability to make any decision for yourself or your loved ones regarding sexual expression, life style, education, religion, economics, politics, aesthetics, etc.

The entrance onto the political scene of totalitarianism is always foreshadowed by the massively destructive plunge into the economic pool of pathologically greedy miscreants who do not or cannot identify with mankind. If nothing constrains the most powerful of these creatures, their toxic ripple grows ever wider.

We cannot help but influence one another and are always doing so. In the marketplace, as long as the nature of our casual or premeditated methods of influence do not descend to methods of interference, we are practicing enlightened self-interest. We are balancing ourselves properly between the savage instinct to grab-the-money-and-run and our social instinct to function in a coordinated manner with other human beings, so that the chances are enhanced for each of us to survive, to reproduce and to bring up thriving families.

A properly run marketplace bears comparison to the rules of chess. Among players who understand the game, chess is a test of skillful subterfuge. Can you disguise well enough from your opponent what you hope will be a sudden and decisive attack? But you must play within the rules, which means you cannot interfere with your opponent. You cannot spike his coffee, hum while he's trying to move, remove or rearrange pieces on the board when he goes to the bathroom, accidentally throw over the board if you are about to be checkmated, etc. If you resort to tricks outside the rules of chess, you have not proven to yourself or to anyone who has knowledge of your forbidden tactics that you are a chess player superior to your opponent or that you have earned any rewards which may result from your victory, even if these are only bragging rights. In addition, it is probably best not to kill or severely maim your chess partners, since you may want to enjoy playing them again. The coldness of logic plods behind the warm vivacity of life. And it is life that must be served, so syllogisms must adjust to their subordinate role as tools within the context of activities invented by living creatures.

A player wins in a game of chess by checkmating his opponent. A businessman triumphs by gaining greater profits than his rivals in order to live better and to demonstrate his superior business skills. And unless he is – in Erich Fromm's terminology – "a culturally patterned psychotic," such as a Corsican gangster, he would not want to kill a rival, and he should realize he would probably be economically better off if every rival did not disappear, as fewer people would be attracted to the commercial area where he operates, diminishing his own profits eventually. Reliable statistics tell us, averaged out over years, rival stores selling similar products in a mall tend to register greater profits than if any one of them over the same period were to operate without competition. Most people who enjoy shopping like to browse, compare bargains to average prices – while factoring in the quality of goods – find accessories, and haggle. They naturally will look for convenient places where the broadest variety of the same category of products is being marketed.

As Adam Smith notes, in the long run monopoly proves itself the least effective way for any proprietor, community or customer to prosper.

Rivals in a marketplace can influence each other appropriately in many ways, some of which are as follows: suddenly marked down products; ballyhooed sales; dependably lower prices on certain goods; bargains to loyal customers; secret formulas that may be patented; carrying fresh, state-of-the-art, novel or better items not in immediate supply to competitors; cost cutting; more effective marketing techniques; hiring more efficient workers; special awards to workers for superior productivity or skill; expanding floor space; opening new outlets; etc.

Unlike the American railroad magnates of the 19th century who regularly tried to interfere with one another by hiring thugs to beat or assassinate rivals or to firebomb their offices, businessmen who value the free enterprise system, must learn to regulate themselves within Smith's laws of justice. If you are both a classical capitalist and a businessman, you will necessarily identify with the community that allows you the resources to develop your profits. Consequently, you will be guided in every instance not so much by how much money you can make, but by **how** you make your money.

Part III

Adam Smith never asserts that there will not be any challenging economic crises if his system were to be adopted. But he does predict that if nations were to voluntarily create among themselves free enterprise zones, common markets, and commonwealths, sustained prosperity for each of them and for every one of their citizens would tend to dramatically increase. One major reason why this would occur relates to the regular economic requirements for defense any country must bear in order to survive. This necessary expense would importantly diminish.

Real threats of war and actual conflicts would not disappear, but their frequency would importantly shrink; a cataclysm that did erupt would tend to be much less profound in its nature and consequences than any war an independent state might normally fight. For every nation that followed the free enterprise plan, in any given armed conflict the extent of territory ravished, the amount of blood and treasure squandered, the portion of time wasted would tend to be considerably less than under any other system. In light of these merits, each realm in harmony with Smith's ideas would gravitate gradually – in concord with all related domains – toward an orbit of lasting peace and prosperity.

But warriors, do not despair. Smith provides a fitting outlet for the warlike tendencies in every one of us. Each independent state would create its own defense force: "…by maintaining and employing a certain number of citizens in the constant practice of military exercises, **it may render the trade of a soldier a particular trade, separate and distinct from all others,"** (Adam Smith, *Wealth of Nations*, Bk. V., ch. I, Pt. i,. p. 660).

Necessarily, this would have to be a voluntary, professional 'standing army,' preferred by Smith for many reasons.

People who might like to soldier, but fear the dangers of the battlefield, would be able to sublimate their bellicose side through participation in violent sports such as boxing, rugby, et al. Today, American football and ice hockey would be included in the same category. Those who could not meet the requirements for either the voluntary armed services or contact sports could still satisfy their lust for blood through the ancient rituals of hunting and fishing. In the 18th century, although not specifically recommended by Smith, they could indulge their cravings vicariously by attending public executions, through watching sporting events or by picnicking near where a battle was being fought, a common entertainment for a civilian population well into the 19th century. To sate our savage tendencies in our own world, society provides active participation in games such as paintball or passive indulgence by listening to violent sports on radio or watching and hearing them on television.

Smith asserts vicarious satisfactions and psychological healing can be gained as well through the entertainments depicted on stage or in novels or epic verse. Sophisticated citizens in our age, find gratification in the great plays of Shakespeare, Ibsen, O'Neil, Williams, et al., the profound novels of Dostoevsky, Tolstoy, Faulkner, etc., the magnificent poetry of Homer, Virgil, Milton, Tennyson and so on. Many fine works of literary art offer the hidden pleasures derived from the portrayal of various kinds of bloodletting, as these works at the same time provide their audiences a catharsis the ancient Athenians, Adam Smith, and Sigmund Freud agreed would make them better citizens. The products of musicians, singers, painters, sculptors, etc. provide similar escapes and spiritual rewards.

Simultaneous with the great decline in military expenditures, pockets of extreme poverty in each nation could then be addressed with greater facility by a particular government or by a council made up of representatives from each country in a particular common market or commonwealth. Adam Smith gives a few hints of what a special program might look like for local areas of poverty. He leaves the rest up to interested students.

In the essay you have in hand and in the Second Section of Part II of Capitalism – the much longer summary and analysis of *Wealth of Nations* that can be purchased from Amazon and other major booksellers – the reader will find my own version of what an effective poverty program should look like in the 21st century. The system is derived directly from contemplation of Smith's concepts.

****

Accommodation, development, preservation, and revival are the essential ingredients of Smith's approach. As liberty accommodates both competition and inventiveness, the profit motive, guided by the laws of justice, will provide occupations, adequate instruction, and a living wage for the masses. And of course a well funded parish would provide proper education to the offspring of every citizen in a given area. Were these conditions constant and pervasive in the affairs of any nation, an ideal state would have been achieved through enlightened self-interest.

But ideal conditions are deemed ideal only because they never or rarely exist. Since men are seldom responsive to more than their immediate needs, they must be guided in the direction of backing the principles and institutions which can be counted on to generate stability and wealth over the long haul. Thus, according to Smith's system of enlightened self-interest, one duty that must be performed by the leader of the nation is erecting and maintaining certain public works and certain public institutions, "which it can never be for the interest of any individual or small number of individuals, to erect and maintain; because the profit could never repay the expence to any individual or small number of individuals, though it may frequently do much more than repay it to a great society," (Adam Smith, *Wealth of Nations*, Bk. IV., ch. ix., p. 651). Smith's assertion encompasses the deliberate development of programs for the masses that would cultivate their evident and potential resources as human beings.

Techniques must be created for the preservation and revival of resources since recessions and depressions will never be entirely eradicated. Economic decline from time to time ought to be contemplated for each part of an economy and for every geographic area of a country. Ergo, rehabilitation insinuates itself as a pivotal theme.

Economic growth is the strategy of capitalism for the initial development of any habitat. Incentives are a major tactic of the free enterprise system in accomplishing initial development and in implementing economic redevelopment when decline has taken place. Smith believed in both economic and psychological revival as a number of passages in his book attest. Thus, not unnaturally, he was also a steadfast advocate of scrupulously fair trials in order to prevent valuable skills and talents from being unfairly removed from the marketplace. However, he tended to be more strident than might be expected in favor of the 18th century's custom of swiftly dispatching any person found guilty of a capital crime. How might certain scientific developments in our own day and age have changed his views?

Smith loved natural philosophy and was very scientific in his methods. He evinced a valuable ability to alter his views in accord with each new scientific discovery. Chemistry was among his foremost scientific interests, so much so that he was instrumental in convincing the University of Glasgow to establish its first chemistry department. These facts alone and his devotion to the cause of justice would have made him delight in the discovery of D.N.A. analysis in the late twentieth century, and his influential voice would have been added to those who oppose the death penalty. Despite such exceptions, the plan laid out and advocated in this treatise is almost entirely derived from the design put forth by Adam Smith in *Wealth of Nations*. Thus it is only fitting that it be presented as an analysis and summary of that great work.

The system could be designated by the use of any agreed upon symbol. However, the history of economics and etymological study strongly suggest that capitalism or classical capitalism or free enterprise or enlightened self-interest be used to refer to Smith's system. I have chosen to use capitalism in my initial references to *Wealth of Nations* because capitalism in the public consciousness would appear to be the term more firmly fixed than any other related to Smith's ideas. Unfortunately, the word has been used indiscriminately to designate just about any economic behavior not specifically socialistic, including all those avaricious practices that have brought about much unnecessary misery. The system itself has been grossly misrepresented by design and by happenstance, by bad example and by poor teaching. It has hardly any passionate advocates outside that small circle of scholars who have made it their business to understand Smith's system.

For decades, the human race has been threatened with total annihilation by means of nuclear catastrophe, which could be triggered by a computer glitch, by the madness of a commanding officer such as General Jack D. Ripper or by the design of an atomic power whose leaders truly believe that Paradise awaits them with its seventy-two virgins if only they can take enough infidels with them in one fell swoop.

Apocalypse could take place any second. Now it takes a mere ten minutes before the point is reached that the missiles cannot be recalled. If it is at all possible to exercise the element known as free will in a way that could have a decisive strategic effect on one's life, it is probably better to choose a long-term pragmatic solution than a short sighted one or one prescribed by a roll of the bones. Many feel the path Adam Smith laid out for us in 1776 is preferable to any other plausible route, as his scheme is built extensively on objectivity, common human decency, and logic. Of course, it might make no difference what we do presently or in the long run.

I believe we can extend the existence of our species by using Smith as our guide to move us in the direction of finding a balance between indulging our chimpanzee appetites and participating in a group effort to secure safety, health, prosperity, liberty, and happiness for the entire community. It would be nice feeling when we arise each morning that our efforts and our taxes were being used at home and abroad to enhance human existence. What a tonic effect on everything we did would this have in the course of each day!

Part IV

No discussion of reform generally would be complete without a review of how our welfare system might be further improved. Citizens currently on the dole comprise people from every racial, religious, and ethnic background. **The following presentation concerning relief <u>can benefit any impoverished group in any nation that wishes to bolster a free enterprise system.</u>**

Adam Smith devotes seven pages to discussing the primitive form of welfare that had evolved in 18th century England, (Adam Smith, *Wealth of Nations*, Bk. I., ch. x., Pt. ii, pp. 135-141). He approves of a net for the poor, but **disapproves of those laws which inhibited or prevented a person from taking up employment which had become available in some other parish.** His complaints sound very similar to ones we still hear about our own welfare system. Undoubtedly, Smith discussed "the poor laws" of England with many manufacturers, mercantilists, and entrepreneurs.

In keeping with the precepts of enlightened self-interest, the best way to defuse the possibility of gnawing poverty becoming revolutionary anger is to provide a sufficient number of well paying, permanent jobs. If some businessman could open up a large enough factory or mercantile outfit to employ all the able-bodied citizens of a particular parish, he would be accomplishing several important things on the economic, political, and social levels: the amount he and other solvent parishioners were in the habit of contributing to support the poor could diminish dramatically because there would be hardly any unemployed left to support in their parish; the net profits from a successful endeavor would fill an owner's personal coffers and allow him to grow his own enterprises and to nurture the ventures of other people, expanding the economy and creating employment opportunities for any number of people. As employment and wealth continued to spread, every conceivable kind of business would be encouraged to open and old businesses would grow; the parishes involved in this delightful process would have many more pockets to draw from for their various building enterprises, educational institutes, widows, orphans, elderly, sick, permanently injured and impaired, etc.; the local, county, and central governments would all have increased taxes from which each member of society could benefit and more money incidentally for the support of endeavors initiated by houses of worship; and so on. **But investment was stymied because the English poor laws would effectively prevent either the opening or the expansion of any kind of enterprise that needed <u>more</u> workers than were available in a particular parish. A citizen taking work in a parish in which he was not originally registered, would find it nearly impossible to get back on the rolls of any parish, including his own, when his job ended.** These obstructive poor laws had to be expunged or corrected because the disorders to which they contributed were "the greatest perhaps of any in the police of England," (Ibid., p. 135).

Smith's ideas about relief are part of the ideology of capitalism. The father of capitalism felt that it is the duty of the central government to protect "as far as possible every member of society from the injustice and oppression of every other member of it, or the duty of establishing an exact administration of justice," (Adam Smith, *Wealth of Nations*, Bk. IV., ch. ix., p. 651). This establishment of an "exact administration of justice" is particularly vital in the area of economics. Within the generous boundaries of his 'speculative work,' Smith invites us to ponder a just welfare system. Obviously one dominated entirely by the voluntary participation of private businessmen practicing enlightened self-interest is preferable to one engineered by government.

However, it is unrealistic to expect businessmen to participate at all without some sort of immediate incentive. The following incentive program would be completely voluntary. Any business could **voluntarily** apply to join and **voluntarily** leave with proper notification. The present system has left millions of people without jobs and without motivation. In accord with the principles of Adam Smith which have been cited and discussed in this essay, a program of incentives ought to be created to solve this most pressing problem.

The particulars of the ensuing discussion fall as well into that same category Smith recognized as needing government participation for the creation of most aspects of infrastructure: "…the duty of erecting and maintaining certain public works and certain public institutions, which it can never be for the interest of any individual or small number of individuals, to erect and maintain; because the profit could never repay the expence to any individual or small number of individuals, though it may frequently do much more than repay it to a great society," (Ibid.).

A welfare bill passed through the U. S. congress several decades ago gave token support to reform. There were more provisions for workfare, which is good because honest work instills a sense of responsibility. However, public taxes pay for almost all workfare because almost all workfare jobs are municipal or county jobs; workfare jobs are invariably in addition to the number of positions that would ordinarily be filled. So our taxes are not reduced, merely shifted, but not shifted away from our wallets. There are more provisions for inducing people on welfare to get jobs in private industry, which is better. More recently in a great number of U. S. communities, legislation has been passed that limits individual welfare benefits to a specific maximum number of years over a lifetime. There are more positive features for everyone than drawbacks in such laws. Many of the ideas regarding welfare in this essay have been implemented already in one form of another by various agencies. I and many other people have been writing for decades about welfare. I only hope that some of what I have written has been useful in the effort to create a better system.

In some measure, our present system of welfare continues to insure an organic gold mine of wealth for The White Powder Kings to plunder and an organic mine shaft of impoverishment for the rest of us. And welfare persists – even in its present state – to demonstrate a basic Marxist formula: "From each according to his own abilities, to each according to his needs." Naturally, people who depend almost exclusively upon the application of this principle tend to develop only socialistic attitudes, which would not be so bad if communism had not proven itself such a totally inadequate system for solving anyone's problems. My present efforts are an attempt to synthesize into one plan what seem to be the most cogent notions concerning welfare reform people commonly talk about. Most of these ideas are in agreement with Smith's economic concepts.

Preliminary to the presentation of my system, I must caution the reader as follows: some people who have read the document you have in hand, have commented that although the incentive part of my plan would no doubt work, as it would considerably lower taxes and premiums, the educational portion of my program would cost a greater amount than the money saved; it would leave us with a more expensive welfare system than we now have. However, this is not correct. Without actually experiencing the plan in operation, this estimation might be true when an insufficient percentage of welfare clientele had been hired – due to catastrophically poor economic conditions. But the above objection needs still further analysis.

The entire progress of mankind – as revealed in its histories, philosophies, religions, its literature, its various arts and sciences – is saturated with the search of each individual and each group for a parental model to follow. Outside catastrophic economic emergencies, when the children of impoverished people see that nearly every adult with whom they come into contact is either gainfully employed or going to school, the attitudes of these youngsters toward work and study will dramatically change for the better. And this POSITIVE IDENTITY TRANSFORMATION (P.I.T.) will diminish the narcotics trade, drug addiction, crime generally, violence, and gang membership to such an extent that annual savings for the public will amount to MANY BILLIONS of DOLLARS. Positive Identity Transformation will make the system I propose by far the least expensive plan for welfare that might ever be established. However, the Capitalist Administration for Relief of Poverty (C.A.R.P.), which will be presented to the reader shortly, must be allowed to come into existence, become fully operational and consistently run for some time – without interference or sabotage – for proper judgment to be rendered as to its effectiveness. I repeat for emphasis, the average per annum expense over years will be far less than we now pay for welfare.

As Senator Proxmire said several decades ago, industrialization or reindustrialization is the only answer to the problem. Since some industrialization once existed in most poor areas, let us stick with reindustrialization. Reindustrialization of welfare areas on an ambitious scale is opposed mainly for three reasons: 1) prejudice. Something our society is still dealing with. 2) unions claim people on welfare would not be able to do jobs in modern industry since all jobs in industry are now "skilled." Unskilled jobs no longer exist. The unions have caused almost all work to be designated as " skilled" in order to raise the price of labor as high as possible, with which I can sympathize. Nonetheless, in reality, 60% of these so called "skilled" jobs can be done by nearly anyone – and this includes nearly anyone on welfare – with a few hours, sometimes a few days, training; 3) the monopolizing spirit of large corporations opposes allowing any bill through congress that would effectively permit enough industry into impoverished city areas to make true reindustrialization possible. Large corporations do not approve of competition – hardly an attitude recommended by Adam Smith. Without the kind of reforms regarding special interests and government suggested in this manifesto, it is unlikely any real progress can be made. However, some token "industrial parks" are being tried in welfare areas. Much more must be done.

The ensuing is a demonstration, as applied to welfare, of the principles and kind of 'speculative' thinking recommended by Adam Smith. I have applied to the problem Smith's concepts of what constitutes a proper stimulus to commerce, supply and demand economics, enlightened self-interest, and the banking system as industry's helper. The program that I propose would be a facilitator of our economy in the same way as the banking system and the stock market. It would fuel competition and existing industry, and it would enable the people on welfare "to provide ... a revenue or subsistence for themselves," (Adam Smith, *Wealth of Nations*, Bk. IV., intro., p. 397). The reader should remind himself as he peruses the present text that **both the modern banking system and the stock markets were**

proposed originally as stimuli and supports for the burgeoning world of business as it was evolving in the seventeenth century.

If proper reform regarding special interests were to take place and to be effectively enforced, the Department of Health, Education and Welfare might be able to eventually contemplate the type of measures presented in this essay. We can only hope for the arrival of such a day.

To make certain that all employable workers benefit from the free enterprise system and not only those who are presently 'useful,' enlightened self-interest urges the creation of a new institution: The Capitalist Administration for Relief of Poverty, whose main purpose would be to replace our present welfare system with a more humane and less costly system.

Specifically, to get people off the dole, with special tax breaks as a first step, C.A.R.P. (The Capitalist Administration for Relief of Poverty) should induce enterprises capable of expansion to open new branches in welfare areas. Any business that desired participation in C.A.R.P. would be **strictly prohibited from reducing in any form or degree** its existing outlets in the economy for purposes of "expansion" through this program. All new outlets in C.A.R.P. would have to be entirely **in addition to what a business already owned and operated.** The reasons for this precondition concern gross tax receipts as will presently become clear. Furthermore, as an additional precaution, no more than 25% of the total of what a particular business manufactured or sold could come from a company's "welfare" outlets at the start of any quarter, unless an exceptional economic crisis was in progress. Wisely administered, the government would create for itself revenues which it could never have gathered without a specially structured program.

Loans at greatly reduced interest rates should be made available for the initial building and equipping of any enterprises in the C.A.R.P. program. The price of money in the past has been lowered for specific purposes only, while interest rates generally have remained at a higher level. Significantly lower interest rates have been used to encourage impoverished minorities to open their own businesses, a practice that ought to continue.

It should be noted that these loans at special interest rates refer just to the initial building and equipping of new C.A.R.P. plants, commercial outlets, etc. This proposal is not intended as a standing offer to these businesses.

For the sake of demonstration, let us say the Federal Reserve Bank interest rate stood at 6% and the prime rate at 9%. 7% would represent a greatly reduced interest rate for C.A.R.P. investments. Bankers would tend to collect more money on interest from loans for the attractive C.A.R.P. program, detailed in succeeding pages, in conjunction with the money on interest from loans made at the ordinary rates, than if loans were made only at the usual rates. Common sense tells us that many more individuals and organizations with the very best collateral and credit ratings would attempt to borrow at 7% for a good investment than at our hypothetical prime rate of 9%. In addition, **such bank loans should be guaranteed by the government.**

Tax breaks for corporations usually benefit the richest, with the public picking up the tab. But the tax break suggested in this essay actually could allow the government to make more in tax revenues with than without the cut, a factor which should lead to reduced taxes for the general public.

Let us imagine that in regard to the possible expansion of existing businesses, given are the following three distinct categories: 1) Solid businesses that definitely have the means to expand, but have **no intention** of doing so. 2) Solvent establishments considering expansion, which have the means to expand, but are **up in the air whether or not to take the risk.** 3) Concerns that have the means and **the clear intention of expanding in the near future.**

In constructing the C.A.R.P. program, the government would create otherwise unattainable revenues for itself **if** the great bulk of investments came from the first of these categories above. Why? Whatever was collected in fresh local, state, and federal taxes from the new outlets would be contributions government **could not have collected** without a special program, as the conservative businesses in the first category have **no intention of expanding as far as anyone can see** under circumstances that might develop naturally.

For the sake of our discussion, let us say every business in the C.A.R.P. program would have to pay only 20% in taxes of what it would pay on the same profits outside the program. **Whatever is collected in revenues from the first category would be gravy.** In addition, any **jobs** the first category might provide would almost certainly never have come into existence. Of course, people presently on the dole would be hired in accord with explicit standards in the C.A.R.P. charter. Without discrete selection the general public might never have the opportunity in relation to these projected businesses to reduce its own taxes tied to the following: (a) reduction in the number of people on welfare; (b) the difference in the pro forma small change removed from each welfare check as taxes and the much larger real contributions former workers on the dole once paid who would again be employed, plus the fresh taxes now paid by new workers who had always been on welfare, having never worked before at any job carried on the books; (c) the additional business revenues of every sort government would never have been able to harvest without the new program.

Those concerns in the **third** category above that have every intention of expanding should be kept at a minimum because whatever might be collected from them in taxes from profits made in C.A.R.P. is a fraction of what would certainly have been collected from the same new profits made outside the program. Of the previously undecided in the **second** category above, those businesses that eventually get to participate in the C.A.R.P. program necessarily resolve themselves into two groups: those that would have expanded on their own regardless of any special program; and those undecided that took the leap ultimately **only** because of the benefits offered by the C.A.R.P. program. Those that would have expanded no matter what, we can combine with the **third** category above. And those that decided to expand in the final analysis **only** because of the special benefits provided by C.A.R.P., we can combine with the **first** category above. Now all these businesses that have actually been chosen to participate in C.A.R.P., through their **voluntary** applications for membership, have been reduced to two groups as follows: (A) businesses that are solid and definitely had the means to expand, **but had no intention of doing so.** (B) concerns that would have expanded **regardless of any program.**

How can any of the above be determined? Government financial experts would have to closely question and go over the books of any business that wanted to join the C.A.R.P. program and such inspection would have to continue for the duration of time an establishment stayed in the program. Any judgments would have to be rendered according to the same standards used to judge applicants for any loan. The financial examiners would not always be correct in their determination of who should be allowed to enter the program, but neither are loan officers in a bank always correct about who should get a loan. Those people making such judgments would simply do the best they could.

Let us look at a demonstration of the simple arithmetic involved in creating such a program. Only small round numbers will be used for the sake of clarity and because my own skill in even the most basic arithmetic leaves much to be desired. Given: (1) As already proposed the C.A.R.P. program requires a participating business to pay only 20% – all taxes combined – of what it would have to pay on the same profits outside the special program. (20% is an arbitrary percentage. Any reasonable percentage appropriate for demonstration will do as well.) (2) Category 'B' above makes $1,000 gross profit from Jan. 1 through Mar. 31 of year X on its establishments in the C.A.R.P. program. (3) Outside the program, 'B' would have been required to pay $300 in taxes on the $1,000 gross profits it made in the C.A.R.P. program.

In the C.A,R.P. program, 'B' must pay 20% of $300, which amounts to $60. From category 'B' in this quarter, the various levels of government all together stand to lose $240, the difference between what they would have collected from 'B' outside the C.A.R.P. program and what they actually collect from 'B' inside the program. **However,** as long as 'B' – **the category of businesses that would have expanded regardless of any program** – contributes no more than 20% to the total taxes collected from C.A.R.P. Jan. 1 - Mar. 31 of the year under consideration, the government would neither make nor lose any revenue for that quarter. Why? If $60 is 20% of the total taxes, then the total taxes from C.A.R.P. for Jan 1–Mar. 31 came to $300, the same amount category 'B' would have paid in gross taxes from its new facilities without any special program. $240 or 80% came from category 'A,' **the category of businesses that would not have expanded without the special program.**

Any percent of the total C.A.R.P. gross taxes for a particular period contributed by category 'B' less than the usual tax break all businesses in C.A.R.P. are receiving, gives the government what amounts to a windfall in taxes. For example, if the $60 paid by category 'B' in our demonstration represented only 10% of the total taxes from C.A.R.P. for a given quarter, the total revenues for that quarter must have come to $600. $540 must have come from category 'A'. Without C.A.R.P., the government would have made $300. With the C.A.R.P. program, the government made 100% more than it would have.

On the other hand, if the $60 collected in taxes from 'B' represented 40% of the total contributions collected from C.A.R.P. for a given quarter, then $150 would represent the total taxes from C.A.R.P. for that quarter. The various levels of government all told would lose one hundred fifty dollars or 50% of what they would have gathered without such a program.

Now one can see the significance of the precondition concerning gross tax receipts mentioned earlier. **(All businesses that wish to build in blighted areas should be encouraged to do so. But after their expansion has been exhausted, C.A.R.P. ought to be instituted).** The difference between an enterprise expanding in C.A.R.P. instead of relocating is the difference between gravy for the tax collector and a loss of revenue because some or all gross profits for a relocated business would be taxed at a lower rate, and the **abandoned**

outlet would no longer generate any taxes. Proportionate to the degree of relocation taking place, if our **national** taxes are to remain adequate year to year, the average citizen ends up with higher taxes than if nothing but expansion takes place. To keep our national taxes at least sufficient to cover necessary expenses year to year, if only or mainly relocation takes place in regard to category 'A' alone, all other factors being equal, the average citizen ends up with a much higher tax bill than before the implementation of the C.A.R.P. incentive program; the little man at this point would be forced to pay that huge portion of taxes the relocated business no longer pays, **added to <u>some</u> costs the abandoned outlets could no longer cover.** Some of these bills would arrive in the form of welfare benefits necessarily paid many laid off workers from the old location(s).The fact most of these freshly unemployed people did not get new jobs would reveal itself – as in decades past – in financial reports, newspaper accounts, and the increasingly loud call for American businesses to return home from abroad. Within the hypothetical context stated above, just the owners of a relocated business would gain since a lower tax bill guarantees higher net profits. But if the-man-in-the-street is to reduce his taxes, real expansion is imperative in the form of totally **additional** outlets in every sense. **This also insures the greatest expansion of employment.** It is mainly through the reduction in unemployment that the little man can hope to reduce his own tax burden. Any **relocated** outlet would hire all their new employees in accord with C.A.R.P. regulations. However, no matter the general condition of the economy, records have suggested 90% of the workers who have been let go from the abandoned locations can be expected to end up on the public dole. By far the lion's share of entitlement comes out of **<u>federal taxes</u>**. The stipends and the former taxes of all the freshly unemployed would then have to be paid largely by each and every one of us.

The savings in taxes just from reduced unemployment would be miniscule because of the welfare benefits now squeezed from the general public to take the place of salaries no longer paid by the abandoned outlets of the corporations in C.A.R.P. Every aspect and detail of speculations about how to reduce the tax bill for the general public must be scrutinized with the utmost care.

Provisions of any bill passed in relation to the above would prevent C.A.R.P. businesses from taking advantage of their much diminished overhead. Should they not be prevented from doing so, these businesses could raise hell via their special situation by reducing prices on some or all their products to such an extent they would **grossly undersell** rivals not fortunate enough to be in C.A.R.P. or an equivalent program and force some into bankruptcy. This could only harm the economy generally in the long run by increasing unemployment and encouraging monopolistic tendencies.

Competitive pricing must be instituted as a matter of law. Except for purposes of a sale lasting a brief period and not repeated for some time, could a C.A.R.P. enterprise steeply lower its price on any competitively sold item. And other than for the cosmetic improvement of an already existing C.A.R.P. unit – C.A.R.P. participants seeking new investments would only be able to use their increased net profits in ventures that had nothing to do with their established outlets in C.A.R.P.

The government would still benefit if a few truly innovative businesses of considerable potential value for mankind did not have to pay any taxes at all from their **expanded** units in C.A.R.P. Capitalism as a politico-economic project must find it beneficial generally to its growth to encourage those especially promising developments that might never have matured without unique consideration. But government spending on welfare would decrease because of indulgence in these expansions, loosening up funds for other things or for lowering the per capita taxes of the entire population. And as already noted in regard to other circumstances, the government would now also be collecting contributions from the previously unemployed, extending the number of people paying taxes. This would also tend to diminish per capita tax burdens. Increased net incomes would help grow the economy.

Stimulus packages appeal, as big plants buy in great quantity at very reduced prices that allow them to sell for comparatively low rates to the public, often forcing smaller retailers and manufacturers to go under. With so many businesses of varying sizes seeking to leave America for Mexico and the Far East in order to reduce their overheads with cheap labor, the methods described herein are a way of keeping businesses in the U.S. and a way of keeping prices down through helping small and middle size concerns that would be able to market some items in their inventories more competitively. This would come about through having diminished their overhead to a significant degree as a result of lower taxes on their new operations in C.A.R.P. Many jobs would be saved and others created.

There are other reasonable solutions to the problem of businesses and jobs moving overseas. When American businesses relocate to foreign countries to obtain cheap labor, most of them send the bulk of their products to the U.S. for sale. As our government has now threatened, through taxation and other economic tools, make certain that the net profits from any and all articles sold on our soil, coming from American factories abroad, amount to less than could have been earned had those same factories remained here. Many establishments have rethought their intentions of moving to another country, and some concerns that had relocated overseas have returned home.

The problem facing Americans of losing jobs to foreign countries has to some small extent been ameliorated by other nations, such as Japan, who have opened factories in the U.S. and have hired American workers. The government should think in terms of creating common markets with Japan, China, Russia, etc. This would tend to aid – without the imposition of an injustice on any group – the greatest possible flexibility about the location of factories, so that – as per proper arrangements in accord with the approved charter – the factory owned by the entity of one state could open or relocate to the soil of another member nation better suiting its needs. Furthermore, an understanding of *Wealth of Nations* among a host of people throughout the world – rather than among very few – would pay dividends for the common man: just consider Smith's hints regarding collective bargaining and his explicit reiterated ideas about a better than living wage **at minimum** for a growing family. Smith considered these as essential stabilizing features of a free enterprise economy.

Smith believed that the need for unions could be greatly diminished by instituting statutes that forced owners to pay as a minimum wage, a living wage appropriate to a particular area, during a specific season. This living wage had to be sufficient to adequately clothe, feed and shelter a growing family, (Adam Smith, *Wealth of Nations*, Bk. I., ch. viii, pp. 67, 68, 74). The minimum wage would rise in pace with the "average price of necessaries," (Bk. V, ch. ii, Pt. ii, Art. 4th, p. 824). The philosopher also opposed all direct taxes upon the wages of labor, (Ibid.)

Wealth of Nations values collective bargaining too, implicit in a number of phrases, including the observation that it was necessary to differentiate between the wages of a skilled and an unskilled worker and between an industrious individual and an average laborer, (Ibid. and Bk. I., ch. x. Pt. ii., p. 142). An owner could increase his own net profits by instituting a just system that would keep workers from unionizing. Also, national unity would increase, lowering the chance of revolution. Work slowdowns, work stoppages, and strikes could be avoided. The burning of factories and warehouses by embittered workers paid starvation wages would disappear. The murder or kidnapping of owners and bosses or members of their families would be averted. A general spirit would emerge that only by group effort could the nation survive.

As an interested reader might imagine, the vehicle intimated by Smith for defense of the workers perhaps would aid in grievances and in all phases of collective bargaining at the end of a specific contract – as do most modern unions.

But attempts at unionization itself, slowdowns, work stoppages, and striking would be forbidden and met with appropriate discouragement. In any legitimate disputes, if it were found necessary, the decisions of a neutral ombudsman would be binding on all parties. A union member hired through C.A.R.P. and fired for cause would have to abide by the rules established by C.A.R.P. or an equivalent group, although a pink slip or any docking of pay could be grieved.

It is obvious, the above measures tend to quell subversion, defuse revolution, diminish the need for unions, and increase generally the wealth of the common laborer so that an individual is able **to buy some of the very products** he has helped to manufacture and to sell. This last factor alone would allow some owners to equal or to surpass in net profits whatever additional overhead they might suffer in wages. For those companies abroad creating expensive conveniences or luxury items, a move back home might be in order.

Although Smith approved of neither unions nor the cruel tactics and conspiracies of owners, as a practical reality, he knew both had to be dealt with, (Adam Smith, *Wealth of Nations*, Bk.I., ch. viii., pp. 66 – 67, et al.).

A larger percentage of welfare checks goes for drugs, alcohol, gambling, etc., than blue-collar or white-collar checks. Disproportionately small amounts go for certain products associated with the middle-class. As the reader will see in the following pages, relatively simple techniques can transform these afflicted welfare districts into blue-collar strongholds; and the newly inculcated values related to stable blue-collar areas will stimulate virtually fresh markets for the products of many businessmen. The corporation that would fall into category 'B' will create for itself increased profits by not obstructing the birth of these additional markets brought to life by the C.A.R.P. program. Increased profits must also accrue as a result of the following: 1) welfare clients and other unemployed people getting relatively decent paying jobs; 2) the additional buying power of everyone because of lower taxes. Our standard of living would tend to go up.

According to the plan which I propose, a large fraction (40% to 66 2/3%) of the workers hired at the very outset for these new extensions would be drawn from unemployed union members of long standing. Thus, the unions would be augmenting their strength from the very outset. Big Labor might find attractive a few of my ideas intended to help management render justice to workers. It is hard to pass laws concerning workers without labor's participation, so any approval is welcome.

Several reasons for including former workers as a large permanent percentage of all the workers hired by C.A.R.P. are as follows: no business can run efficiently without a great deal of experience at every level. One of the main reasons for choosing to hire individual **A** over individual **B** is that individual **A** has more experience working the kind of job being offered. People who have worked before can set an example for people who have never worked before. And the experienced man can give detailed instructions to a novice. Thus, net profits can be made greater than they would have been without the availability of experienced hands. Besides, as a result of the pandemic and manufacturers moving abroad, there are nearly as many former workers that remain union members presently on the dole as people who never had a job. So it would be difficult to obtain a complete work force without including many of these experienced hands.

One can see how our taxes would be diminished. Taxpayers, the reader should be reminded, also pick up the tab for the amount of taxation no longer paid by laid off workers and must pay additionally the welfare of those who have used up their unemployment benefits.

What should be the nature of the tax break? As this essay has already speculated, a business which opens an additional branch in a poverty stricken area should pay in taxes in the vicinity of 20% of what it would have to pay, all taxes combined, from that particular plant in any non-welfare neighborhood. As per stringently enforced legislation, in order to get this special break, a business would have to adhere to the following proviso: no less than 50% of what it would have had to pay in taxes in another area be used strictly to hire or train those people from the poverty area who either are on welfare or are headed for the welfare rolls. (When this 50% amounts to more than a particular company needs to pay the wages **of those they have already employed from welfare**, to hire new workers from present welfare rolls or to train those people from the poverty area for its own shop, the excess will go into a fund to be used for any purpose within the C.A.R.P. system deemed appropriate by appointed C.A.R.P. executives).

When a branch opened initially, law would prescribe that no less than one third to no more than three fifths of the original regular employees be from welfare clientele who were **non-union** members and from ghetto youths not yet on welfare. (The fraction would not be allowed to dip below one third during the life of any C.A.R.P. unit). As many **specialists** as 26 2/3% of all workers employed can be hired from anywhere if the worker minimums allowable are hired from the non-union and union welfare clientele, respectively 33 1/3% and 40%. **But C.A.R.P. would not allow any factory in the program to switch to automation, except where it had been clearly demonstrated that no welfare clientele or unemployed crew or individual worker(s) not yet on relief could adequately master whatever skills were necessary to get a particular job done.** The program described herein is meant to relieve poverty, not stick a thumb in the eye of poor people. Except for vital areas such as defense, perhaps law ought to limit **all automation**.

Many factories have sales offices and some also have distribution departments. As many welfare clients as possible should be hired to fill sales positions and jobs in distribution. If the 50% figure mentioned above can only be reached by hiring people for chores in the shop itself, the excuse that automation has already filled the available spots will not be accepted. Even if the entire manufacturing area of a C.A.R.P. plant had only human workers, the amount of the tax break on profits would be adequate to allow competitive pricing to take place. But these subtle calculations ought to be estimated in advance by C.A.R.P. lending officers before letting a particular manufacturer into the program. For example, if a furniture manufacturer that wanted to be in the program might have to compete against a fully automated furniture manufacturer outside C.A.R.P., the financial experts would have to turn down the potential borrower on the basis he would never be able to lower his prices sufficiently to be competitive and make a reasonable profit. But even were this rare situation described above to come about subsequent to a particular manufacturer succeeding in the program or because of miscalculation by C.A.R.P. bankers, the manufacturer in the program would be able to automate up to the point where he could sufficiently lower his prices to be competitive while making a sound profit.

The procedures for laying off trainees and temporary help would follow the appropriate union contract. Under the new system expounded in this essay, anyone hired directly from welfare, who subsequently lost the position for which he was originally employed, would immediately and automatically be placed back on the relief program in existence at that time, so long as the reason for being fired was not the result of some unusually counter-productive behavior such as constant lateness or chronic absence from work without a verifiable excuse. (See Leonard M. Greene, *Free Enterprise Without Poverty*, New York, 1981).

The wages of regular employees should be at the current rate paid for that particular job in non-welfare areas of the same county or state and would keep pace with the wages paid for such a job.

If the taxes from these complexes reached a certain level, the taxes alone taken by the government from these "welfare" shops might be enough to support the program for those for whom jobs still had not been found and who were not in training. At that point, welfare stipends could be allowed to fluctuate with the varying profits of C.A.R.P. from period to period – to the extent these proceeds reflected the national economic picture. Everyone's tax burden would tend to be more significantly reduced under the conditions stated above than it would be reduced at other times C.A.R.P. was in operation. **However, at no time would this reduced tax burden be slight.**

To insure to some extent that all the jobs offered are taken by members of a designated community, the employees hired first of those qualified should be the ones who could financially benefit most from working as opposed to being on the welfare rolls. In fact legislation should provide that each new employee from the poverty area be given a net salary that is at least 20% greater than what he could net on welfare either because the pay actually amounts to that much or because the government has subsidized his check up to that 20% point; this ought to be the procedure related to any job taken by a welfare recipient as long as it ultimately resulted in lower taxes. The supplement would fluctuate with the wage and disappear when an individual's wage reached a point at which it was 20% more net than he would make on welfare at that time. (Cost, including the expense of child-care, would decide each case for job provision, wage supplementation or relief. As some communities are now doing, anyone on welfare who rejects a job, without a certifiable reasonable excuse, would have his stipend sharply reduced or eliminated. This would help diminish the number of people on the dole who simultaneously worked at a job off the books.). This last point is not meant as a rebuke to the struggling poor.

Strictly within the parameters of what an employer would otherwise have to pay into the C.A.R.P. fund, he would have little reason to quibble about most wages. However, these same parameters bring other limiting factors into play. To the average taxpayer, at first glance it looks attractive to hire as many people as possible off the welfare rolls. But since the taxpayer has to make up a C.A.R.P. employee's net pay until it is 20% more than he can make on welfare, at a certain point – factoring in what the taxpayer would have to continue contributing for all workers in the pool of people who could be hired for the same job – in certain circumstances it might make more sense to hire fewer people, each at a greater salary, than more people, each at a lower wage. But this would probably have little weight in the hiring decisions of an employer.

In order to moderate between the needs of management and the just claims of big labor, if a private business must close extensions because of cutbacks, a fair plan should always be followed. But C.A.R.P. outlets by statute during a national economic emergency **would be the very last to close**. (Due to special tax breaks, these shops in all likelihood would be the most profitable of the several branches of an enterprise, proportionate to the amount of business conducted by each unit). This procedure might allow the non-welfare outlets to reopen eventually, which would possibly have never reopened without this complete program and would have closed earlier than they did in actuality.

The welfare program of a free enterprise system, in accordance with Smith's thoughts, should be constructed around the concept of relieving whatever poverty develops in the nation at a given time, with the pivotal notion of keeping the economy stable during any period of severe crisis. A new investor drawn from a list of companies that were ready to participate in this process would replace any welfare extension forced to close. This would allow the welfare communities to naturally ebb and flow with the tide of the national economy. In the ultimate analysis, during an officially recognized crisis, a welfare facility should be the very last to close because without a buffer zone, a severe or very extended recession or moderate depression could destroy the very program intended to stabilize the country while recovery takes place. And this built-in program might spell the salvation of the free enterprise system itself within a given context.

As noted, legislation would also force products from "welfare" shop companies to be sold at competitive prices. Those outlets established in or near the poverty areas for no less than six months prior to initial passage of the proposed legislation will receive compensation if they are in direct competition with one or more of these new "welfare" shops. This compensation applies to just the approximate type and amount of inventory in direct competition with items handled by **the new C.A.R.P. enterprises** on their opening day or subsequently. The previously established concerns will not be compensated by selling a product in direct competition with an item **featured first** by a C.A.R.P. business. Compensation will continue only for the original type and proportionate amount that is maintained as part of the inventory or until such time as either the established shop or the new C.A.R.P. outlet ceases to sell the same item(s). If a C.A.R.P. shop went back to selling a discontinued item, compensation would begin again.

The following is one possibility for the fair compensation mentioned above in regard to the previously established businesses in the area: Each of their quarterly taxes could be reduced by a certain amount on the profits only from the sale of those items in direct competition with the products produced by or sold by the new C.A.R.P. outlets. This reduced tax should be the amount that would allow these items to be retailed at competitive prices. Additional tax credits could be given to those directly competing, long established firms for each welfare client they subsequently hire, if such is not already the case.

However, there is very little in these blighted areas with which C.A.R.P. would be competing. Where there are a few original factories still in operation, the chiefs of C.A.R.P. could simply **not** allow a competing factory to open in the area. The same selective process could be used in the choice of wholesalers and retailers.

Furthermore, if any business not a part of this program – which operates inside or outside a designated impoverished area where C.A.R.P. has been establishing itself – feels that it is losing profits as a result of the C.A.R.P. program – there is nothing to prevent this same business from applying to the proper sources for entrance into the C.A.R.P. program itself, thereby helping to relieve poverty in a capitalistic manner.

Why can't people now on welfare be employed in already existing businesses according to the same general principles laid down in this manifesto?

There are several reasons. Many people on the dole have become addicted to their privileges. In addition, the approximately twenty square miles known as the South Bronx, which is now being rebuilt to some degree, remains to large measure a typical welfare area that is blighted. There are presently few factories in this section of New York City; they employ a handful of people. Commerce exists mainly in the form of small, family owned stores. Large retailers have closed up and moved away due to the prevalence of violent crime. No jobs are available. Why can't these welfare clients be employed in businesses outside the poverty area? Some have, but there are relatively few jobs open for people without skills, and for jobless union members with specific skills, the positions have already been filled. Additionally, welfare beneficiaries are reluctant to take any job carried on the books, no matter how profitable the weekly net profits for such a position may be, because of the near impossibility of getting back on welfare if employment is lost. They would be without any means of surviving. This same problem plagued workers in Smith's day because of the 'poor laws'.

What about workfare? As suggested earlier, workfare is punitive, and we still have to pay the exact same taxes for workfare as we now pay for welfare. Workfare jobs are municipal or county positions, which consist of bits regular employees would do in the course of a day's work or during slack periods without additional pay. The program detailed in this manifesto greatly diminishes our tax burden.

One reason why businessmen resist the kind of social and economic equation that the solution in this treatise presents is the memory of the enormous financial losses incurred during the race riots of the nineteen-sixties. In 2015 and 2016 these fears were reawakened. Racial stereotypes and prejudices were reinforced. However, there is evidence that many of these disturbances were initiated by individuals employed by racists, by hostile foreign entities or the underworld. Only narcotics salesmen, racists, communists and other totalitarians benefit from the wonton destruction of property in inner-city neighborhoods. Nevertheless, signs persist that things are changing for the better. The vision of an industrial/commercial complex in each of the welfare communities of America remains a practical means of attaining social tranquility along the most just and democratic lines.

Any community conscious of the fact that many of its present and future jobs and a portion of its financial benefits for those who remain unemployed depend upon the profits and taxes from the factories and other businesses in the complex, will do everything within its power to maintain the security of the complex. Necessarily, this would entail an intense effort by the community to combat the drug problem.

According to the needs of a particular business or group of enterprises, as is the case in suburban areas, the C.A.R.P. outlets would be protected from thieves and saboteurs by a variety of choices, which could be combined: cameras, alarms, special locks, gates, stone walls, cyclone fences, trained dogs, security guards, night watchmen, etc. Some part of the expense for the security system might have to come out of city, state, and federal taxes. This cost to the taxpayer would be a piffling amount when measured against the immense overall benefits of the C.A.R.P. program to specific municipalities, to the states in which these cities exist, and to the entire nation.

To offset this expense in large part, the very first sort of enterprise C.A.R.P. directors should seek to expand into the C.A.R.P. program are a sizable company providing security and one or more very large construction companies; these firms by law would do all the building necessary for themselves and any enterprise entering the program in their area. The corporation dealing in matters of security would provide the personnel and equipment for itself and for each and every business in C.A.R.P. related to that particular impoverished district. An abundance of workers from welfare could be hired for jobs in construction and as guards in security.

Other factors make the C.A.R.P. program appealing: 1) Whatever expenses for security, in the initial stages of setting up the program, the cities, states, and central government had to provide could be reimbursed in part by the fund, which has been mentioned. 2) Furthermore, any municipality or group of C.A.R.P. enterprises that chose to do so could buy up the area immediately surrounding the complex to provide low income housing exclusively for the people employed on a permanent basis in the C.A.R.P. program.

Finally, from a host of practical details that might be suggested, let me recommend but two: a) Just as bus and train passes are provided to school children so that they are able to use the transit system free of charge, the same could be done for any workers in the complex who wanted to live outside the immediate area where they were employed. b) And, as is now done in many work facilities throughout the U.S., the cafeterias of the complex could serve food at cost.

As will be seen more clearly in the succeeding pages, the welfare system, as it now exists, would continue in use only for those people that from the commencement of the C.A.R.P. program were unable to work because of age or physical or mental disabilities. Their stipends would continue for life.

****

Preparatory to making any recommendations about what C.A.R.P. should do as a next step, it might be useful to contemplate what ought to be done with a mass of jobless people who have exhausted their unemployment benefits with all the reasonable extensions of these benefits government would allow – while they search for jobs which perhaps do not exist and show little sign of materializing. Place them in a W.P.A.-type program, repairing buildings, homes, walls, sidewalks, roads, trails, rails, paths, parks, woodlands, tunnels, bridges, canals, etc., which need work, but stand little chance of ever being repaired by municipal, county or private employees. There are plenty of the aforementioned tasks that need to be done. This would significantly help the economy.

As the stimulus section of C.A.R.P. develops and provides positions for welfare recipients, this same agency would also provide jobs for people now on the W.P.A. part of their unemployment benefits. Of course provisions would be made for these people to go on job interviews when appropriate openings showed up. Such procedures will save the taxpayer for an appreciable time from the greater cost of placing these currently unemployed people on welfare. Now let us turn our attention once again to welfare proper.

It might surprise some readers to know, a number of people collecting full relief benefits are also gainfully employed in the private sector part time and even full time. However, they labor at jobs **not carried on the books and these positions are not recorded officially,** so the welfare stipends of these people are unaffected. These citizens would never take any work carried on the books even if they could net many times what they could collect on welfare. They would refuse such an offer for the following reasons detailed several decades ago in *Free Enterprise Without Poverty*: anyone who took a job that officially listed him on a payroll would have deductions made for social security, taxation, retirement benefits, et al. The individual, according to law, would naturally have to forfeit his welfare benefits. And were a person in the course of time to lose his position **for any reason,** it would be virtually impossible to get back on relief. Such an individual would be left destitute. So before the stimulus section of the C.A.R.P. program got under way, it must be explained clearly that anyone who took a position offered by C.A.R.P., who subsequently lost his or her job, would be immediately placed **back on the welfare rolls with full benefits,** so long as dismissal had not been the result of something akin to extreme absenteeism without a legitimate, verifiable reason.

All those people who currently collect welfare should be engaged in adult education programs. Such a procedure will prepare some people who have never worked for their first job. This method has been tried on a small scale with considerable success in various parts of the United States and abroad.

Social workers ought to be required to have fulfilled two majors while in college: the major built around the usual courses in sociology; and a major or a minor built around a subject to be taught. For example, any of the following would be an appropriate area: one of the art fields (creative writing, music, painting, acting, dress design, et al.); one of the pragmatic courses (English, English as a second language, secretarial studies, computer programming, accounting, business administration, nursing, and so on); or one of the areas usually referred to as shop (carpentry, construction, plumbing, upholstering, auto mechanics, bartending, etc.) A major or minor in education should be required in order to prepare these social worker/adult educators for giving classroom instruction. Social workers now employed could begin teaching courses for which they met the requirements, while they took appropriate education courses. Public school teachers could be hired and any properly trained retired person could be employed again.

C.A.R.P. should make people on welfare aware of what kinds of skills may be required of them in the new jobs being created. Adult education programs should be offered in all these areas. But since many of the positions to be filled would require little or no training and because a long wait for a job may occur, the program must not be restricted to narrowly utilitarian goals. Although everyone on welfare would be required to enroll and attend some course of study, no one would be required to take a class he or she did not want. Courses or entire educational tracks could be repeated or switched at the end of each semester with proper notification. C.A.R.P. would proceed to discover by simple routine questioning and testing what people who remain on welfare like to do or had the skill to do. The new welfare system would pay people on a graduated scale relative to the quantity and quality of their products and their attendance in appropriate classes. For example, a man now on welfare claims that he likes to write poetry. He enters an adult education program in poetics, along with other like-minded people, instructed by a person qualified in the area of versification. He is paid 50% of his monthly stipend on the basis of consistent attendance, 45% on productivity, and 5% on quality as judged by his instructor(s) or some outside authority. The poet would retain ownership of his work, be taught how to copyright his material, and of course could sell his poetry independently. At least the skill and knowledge of the mechanics of verse could be checked and improved. He must produce a specific number of words per month to get 45% of his base payment, let us say. Production earns him more each step of the way through a series of plateaus to a ceiling of 5,000 words. The quality of the mechanics, according to certain explicit standards of which he has been carefully informed, earns him additional income.

The central welfare office through which C.A.R.P. would be working, would also provide him with such fundamental essentials as pencils, pens, writing pads, as per reasonable request, and perhaps even a glossary of literary terms. But the central office would not provide typewriters, computers, a rhyming dictionary, thesaurus or other expensive products, although such items could be used free of charge within the educational institutions attended by any adult in the program. Anyone who feels that he can increase his earnings by investing in equipment or aids of one sort or another is learning how to invest money to make money, which is proper in a free enterprise economy. As noted, barring of course some certifiable extenuating circumstance, such as a death in the family, et al. – no one could receive a welfare check who had not produced the base amount required. These above suggestions in no way preclude the present provisions for dependents as they now exist in welfare, i.e. the top payment for someone with one dependent would equal the base check of someone with several dependents. But it should be stipulated by law that any female placed on the welfare rolls will continue to be paid appropriate welfare benefits **only** for those children she already had and with which she was pregnant at the time of being listed for benefits. **Her stipend will not increase by a single penny for any child she becomes pregnant with after joining welfare.** In this regard, the current rules encourage self-destructive behavior, behavior which harms as well the surrounding community and the general economy, without any redeeming long term benefits for anyone. Our tax burden increases because of this single piece of faulty legislation perhaps more than for all the other pieces of faulty legislation combined that are associated with welfare. Of course all the methods of birth control should be offered free of charge at clinics for any individual collecting benefits.

The versifiers alluded to above should be required to produce a class or school poetry magazine and encouraged to produce poetry magazines or books of verse outside the classroom and to organize poetry workshops for readings and to sell their works curbside. These recommendations, where appropriate, also apply to people engaged in the other arts: novel and playwriting, journalism, etc., painting, sculpting, music, dance, et al.

Up to a certain point, profits these people generate for themselves while on welfare should not be subject to taxation. Should they generate enough income to make themselves independent of welfare, this will reduce public taxation. But even were these sources to remain hidden from the government, **whatever** money is generated will be spent, saved or invested, and these activities will help local communities and the general economy. As a supplement to welfare checks, small cash prizes and plaques should be given at the end of each stipulated period of time for the best products in each field, (Adam Smith, *Wealth of Nations*, Bk. IV., ch. v, p. 489). Sports leagues for baseball, handball, billiards, hockey, basketball, football, etc. could be formed on a similar basis. Chess, checkers, and card-playing leagues could also be developed.

Although they could do so **voluntarily**, people on welfare should **not** be **required** to search for employment. This has never worked in the past, and there is little chance such a requirement will ever work in the future for reasons already given – unless there are significant changes in the law. All job offers for welfare recipients should be funneled through C.A.R.P. When a job becomes available for a welfare client, the individual should be chosen according to the person's suitability for the position offered and the extent to which the public's tax burden would be lightened.

With such satisfying activities to perform as described above, why should any welfare client take a job that is offered? There are a number of reasons: 1) The work offered, as noted, would pay 20% more **net** than the individual could collect on welfare. 2) The total amount of time a person can spend on welfare in now strictly limited in most states. 3) Under this program, any person hired from welfare who lost his position would immediately be placed back on welfare with full benefits, so long as he had not been fired for extreme absenteeism, constant and aggravated tardiness or some form of unusually inexcusable behavior at work. The brilliant educator Meryl A. Volpe has said in private conversation regarding this problem: "**No person now on welfare who takes a C.A.R.P. position or finds work himself should be removed from the welfare rolls.** Whatever he or she received from welfare would fluctuate with the need to see that the net pay for each month amounted to 20% more than the individual could make on relief alone at that time. This 20% supplement would also apply to all benefits that would now come from whatever company hired him. But while he or she was employed, the time would **not** be subtracted from the maximum number of years the individual was allowed to spend on the dole in a particular area of residence." (This procedure would reduce the fear of taking up work.) 4) In his spare time, before or after work, a person could continue whatever he had been doing for his welfare stipend. And whatever additional income he earned on his own would be gravy. 5) Finally, to refuse to take a job offer without a verifiable legitimate reason would be met with a sharp reduction of benefits or removal from the welfare rolls.

****

Wouldn't the facilities required for adult education and activities such as football or baseball be exorbitant? Let the incentive section of C.A.R.P. get started first so that enough fresh funds will have been generated – from the new sources and the reduced cost of entitlement – to allow the education section of C.A.R.P., at its outset, to be adequately financed. As little money as possible should be taken from public coffers as they would stand before accommodation of the C.A.R.P. program. Some functional structures would have to be erected, but this initial cost would be a trifle compared to the immense amount of money saved once this program got under way.

Furthermore, were the public to be taxed for preparing sports fields, the contributions would be an iota of the taxes we now pay for very roughly equivalent categories related to welfare as it presently exists. But these things need not cost even that iota. Give clients their checks in part for creating the playing fields and for supervising the activities whenever it is feasible to do so. Many acres of these poverty areas remain empty lots. (Cities may be required to provide some soil for covering playing fields).

The proper number of prefabricated one story or two story buildings, each covering several acres, containing many properly equipped classrooms, several bathrooms, offices, a library, an auditorium, and boiler room can be built at very little public expense, each structure serving the academic needs of fifteen to twenty thousand adult students following staggered daily programs. People now on welfare can be hired as construction workers, security guards, paraprofessionals, secretaries, monitors, janitors, et al. Whatever the costs for mechanical and material supplies will have to come out of public taxes, but these costs will be more than compensated by the taxes no longer needed to cover the expenses incurred handling all the facile and widespread cheating that characterizes welfare now. Under the new system proposed, fraud will diminish rapidly and naturally to a bare minimum.

Over time the entire C.A.R.P. program would be much cheaper to run than our current costly and destructive welfare scheme, for the following seven reasons: 1) Under normal economic conditions, the number of people hired from welfare through the stimulus section of C.A.R.P. would greatly diminish the number of people left to be taught in the adult education area of the program, importantly lowering public taxes. 2) As increasingly fewer students had to be instructed, more attention could be paid to each pupil, increasing the ability of each person to learn. This would tend to increase the ability of each adult to make money. 3) There would be fewer people necessary to run all aspects of the C.A.R.P. program than are now necessary to run all aspects of welfare in its current form. As fewer social worker/adult educators became necessary, retirement alone would provide cost effective attrition. 4) Even though some prefabricated school buildings would be an expense, **it is a one-time cost,** not a recurrent bill. 5) School supplies for the adult education program would be supplied through boards of education which would buy in greater bulk than they now do, but in doing so would lower the average price for each item purchased. And none of these cheaply bought purchases should ultimately go to waste, regardless of the ultimate fate of the C.A.R.P. program, because in any event they could be used by the regular school system. 6) In an economic crisis, unemployment would increase, and more people would end up on the education side of C.A.R.P. And although these fresh bodies would have to be supplied with books, pens, etc., the public treasury would not have to support an increase in staff size. Only the number of students per class would suffer increase, until the economy was stabilized once again. 7) To repeat a point already made, when children and teenagers realized almost the entire adult population in their neighborhoods was either employed or going to school, they would gain a much greater respect for work and for education. Drug use, violence, and crime would decrease dramatically, saving citizens an ocean of money in taxes and insurance rates. This phenomenon would be an example of the effects of Positive Identity Transformation elucidated earlier.

The proposed legislation should also give people who remain out of work **after their welfare allowances have run out**, half of what they got on welfare under the condition of continuing in the adult education program as before. C.A.R.P. would continue to search for jobs these people were able to do.

An entirely new kind of culture issues from this novel organization. An individual involved in this type of community must learn self-discipline because he must produce a certain number and quality of a given product within a stipulated period of time. The hours of the twenty-four hour day suddenly become important. He must spend a certain portion of his time laboring to produce what provides him income. Implicitly, he is learning about fair competition for profit. He is becoming a member of the free enterprise community.

Beyond these essential points of organization, the individual gains enormously in self-respect because his products and his innate abilities are the essence of what allows him to survive. He is no longer being given something for nothing. He is no longer being paid to remain nothing. His abilities have been recognized and their development is being rewarded. The various talents of anyone on welfare will have the opportunity of being displayed and appropriately reinforced. And what will issue from the proper cultivation of these talents is similar to what issues from the proper cultivation of a patch of earth that had been left fallow. Given appropriate amounts of water and sunlight, fresh shoots of every sort flower and flourish. A cultural Renaissance evolves. And what was perhaps in some instances an eyesore becomes a showcase of what free enterprise at its best is capable of doing. Anyone on the dole who refuses to participate or attempts to sabotage the proceedings will have to subsist on a very reduced stipend.

Are there drawbacks to such a system? Of course. But they are outweighed both in number and substance by the advantages. This program is far superior to our present welfare system, and far better than having no system at all for the relief of poverty, a situation that would swiftly lead to chaos and to the establishment of a totalitarian state of one sort or another.

In the light of present realities, certain tactics once used by welfare are of value. For example, restoration should be made of the procedure whereby the system pays rents directly to landlords for those on the dole. There is at least a moderate correlation between non-receipt of rent checks and tenement blazes. And a substantial part of their monthly allotments should be paid people on relief in the form of coupons and stamps requiring signatures and proper identification with purchases. This would tend to eliminate mailbox theft by addicts, and it would help to eliminate the use of stipends by recipients for illicit drugs, alcohol, and gambling. Ultimately, the federal government ought to impose the degree of regulation herein suggested over the system, no matter what its final form, in order to make standard the cumulative time any person or family can spend on welfare and to make welfare payments uniform throughout the U.S. These aspects would tend to keep people in their native states and communities. The decrease in traumatic relocations proportionately increases positive familial and community ties. Moreover, the burden of such payments would no longer fall on those cities and states that offered the highest welfare benefits or allowed the greatest amount of cumulative time on the dole, overwhelming these communities in the long run.

Why should the average citizen care about the proposals contained in this essay? Were my recommendations concerning the C.A.R.P. program put into effect, the following would ensue: (a) The taxes of everyone would significantly and permanently diminish. (b) Insurance premiums would significantly decrease. (c) Safety in every area of our cities and towns would vastly improve. (d) Dangers to the physical and mental health of the general public would appreciably decline. (e) We would have a demonstrably positive and coherent politico-economic philosophy to export that would help bring us together with other nations, and thus diminish the chances of unnecessary conflicts.

As a result of the ideas in this essay being put into effect, the general wealth, security, and happiness of the entire nation would increase importantly over the long haul. All the normal activities that occur between economic and political entities will continue as before, but on much firmer ground. The competition between the various political parties will continue more vigorously than in the past perhaps, since public confidence in government would be restored, as certain nagging problems will have been adequately addressed. Because many more people will have fatter wallets than in the past, old businesses will expand and new ones will come into existence, creating more vigorous and more healthy competition than ever before. Under the vast and sturdy umbrella proposed in this treatise, all business factors, all differences of opinion, all political conflicts, and all religious disputes will have an even playing field upon which to compete. Moreover, all of the above will be done in harmony with the precepts of the free enterprise system and will bolster that system. Per example, a stimulus program in accord with Adam Smith's ideas will have been instituted, while doing what essential supply and demand economics is supposed to do:

stabilize and expand the economy; over time this will help create as much profit as possible for the private sector and spur the private sector to gainfully employ as many citizens as possible; a program for developing the talents of those who remain unemployed will help to make these people more likely to become economically independent. Finally, a collective unconscious of free enterprise will be created by the efforts of everyone working together.

The people opposed to the concepts developed in this essay maintain the idiotic view that everything I have written actually leads to socialism. Before anything else, let us unpack this absurd allegation. Since the middle of the 19th century, certain ideas that lend balance to classical capitalism have been considered the seeds of socialism. No doubt this assertion is true. But Smith was no socialist.

The systems of socialism and communism came to fruition in the **19th century.** The words socialism, socialist, communism, and communist first found print in the **19th century. Smith last revised *Wealth of Nations* personally for its fifth edition in 1789 shortly before his death in 1790.** All his ideas about poverty and the fate of the average man came from Smith's scholarship, his notions of justice, and his own common sense. If you wanted a stable politico-economic scheme that avoided the kind of unrest that led to violent revolution, the common man had to be reasonably treated.

The really stupid exclamation that we ought to be concerned about the way capitalism is practiced today, deserves the following response: Smith invented classical capitalism, which very few people bothered to either study or to take seriously, except for a few professors who had neither clout nor capital, so their warnings were brushed aside as so much smoke. No person or government consciously practiced classical capitalism. It was as though an individual had created the game of chess, and everyone who claimed to understand the game, went ahead and played some form of checkers. After all Smith's tome is nine-hundred pages long, written in well-turned eighteenth century phrases, dry as dust. When some jackass begins to talk about 'late capitalism', he or she is actually referring to 'mercantilism', precisely the system Smith fought so vigorously. 'Late capitalism' or mercantilism is depicted as a plan in which there is little or no competition and business is conducted between gigantic, privately owned monopolies. This is like an anthropologist saying that humans have been evolving from modern man who first appeared about fifty thousand years ago, and *homo sapiens* have descended so far that we are developing coarse black hair all over, prognathous jaws, little beady eyes, exceedingly long arms, and the necessity to balance ourselves on the knuckles of our hands when we come down from our arboreal retreats.

Adam Smith asks his students to ponder and elaborate his politico-economic philosophy contained in *Wealth of Nations.* Like many people before me, I have bent to the task. Since Adam Smith makes it abundantly clear that he is much in favor of universal education, in Part IV, I have taken this as one of my jumping off points. Perhaps, Smith's most trenchant remarks about education can be read in the following: "An instructed and intelligent people besides, are always more decent and orderly than an ignorant and stupid one. … In free countries, where the safety of government depends very much upon the favourable judgment which the people may form of its conduct, it must surely be of the highest importance that they should not be disposed to judge rashly or capriciously concerning it," (*WN*, Bk. V., ch. I, Pt.iii, Art. 2nd, p. 740). Smith discuses the education of children and the improvement of university instruction. I have extended his observations to adult education and added some of my own.

Many arrogant and almost magically ignorant individuals claim to represent true capitalism since they deal exclusively in investments – without the slightest regard for Smith's laws of justice. The sufferings even of their own people are of little importance to them, much less the sufferings of other nations. They are members of that same reptilian species who for profit alone manipulated the various markets to bring us the First World War, **the communist revolution**, the Great Depression, National **Socialist** Germany, the Second World War, the Holocaust, **the Soviet takeover of Eastern Europe**, **the Cold War**, the Great Recession, etc. For none of these events will they accept the slightest responsibility.

Were any of these people aware of the contents of *Wealth of Nations*, which many scholars commonly refer to as "the bible of free enterprise"? Presuming a few read the book, did any of them understand it? If a tiny number comprehended the text, did any one of them care? Of those who might have given a damn, it must have been the murderous nature of the organizations they labored for that forced their silence about all those unreasonable restraints of fair trade which invariably led to international catastrophe.

In the long run, most of these ravenously selfish people were shortsighted even in reference to their own fates. Their mantra remains life is short and you only go around once; so the best way to get the most out of your brief existence is to be totally ruthless. A mere handful who follows this dictum ever prosper by it. It is the kind of prescription handed out by Stalin's NKVD to sow discord, and more than a few brokers and bankers who subscribed to it were fully aware of how their behavior would nurture the communist conspiracy.

The measures favored in this essay do not have to be passed in one fell swoop. They can be passed incrementally over time. And none of them are written in stone. They are presented to the reader for **contemplation. They can be refined or improved or modified or entirely jettisoned,** but if they are rejected, they ought to be replaced by concepts which evince a better promise of achieving the same common goals as the discarded notions.

However, I believe were all my suggestions put into effect, an unmanageable situation will have been transformed into one that was manageable, one we could all live with. Anything beyond that would be gravy. Furthermore, we would of course continue to be plagued by difficulties because economics is a part of life and life by definition means problems, many of which we cause ourselves through an exercise of arrogance or envy or spite or obsequiousness. And the person is correct who says "You will never get rid of corruption or organized crime." We never will get rid of these things *entirely* because they issue from an ineradicable part of human nature, and it is preferable **not** to get rid of these features completely. But we must at least try to reduce certain self-destructive aspects of humanity to a level commensurate with bare survival. The scheme described above for relieving poverty gives us identity, strength, and unity around a model both plausible and positive. It has an extraordinarily good chance of succeeding if it is not effectively sabotaged.

The only principles worthy of being categorized as moral effectively protect the survival of society over time. For most of the time 'modern man' has paced this earth, he has been directed by individuals who cared only for themselves and their own families. It was the rare leader indeed who cared enough to make any sacrifice for the common good or knew how to direct others to help a culture to endure.

A person who in every instance believes what is best for himself is identical with what is best for the state is a moral cretin. Those people are moral cretins who practice the original *laissez-faire* economics created in the 18th century by Dr. Quesnay and given the royal imprimatur by Quesnay's patient – King Louis of France.

The legal profession bears some measure of responsibility for many of the economic difficulties which have beset civilization. In America, an entire year of law school – preferably the first year – should be strictly dedicated to studying *The Articles of Confederation, The Declaration of Independence, The Federalist Papers, The Constitution of the United States, The Theory of Moral Sentiments, Wealth of Nations*, the various essays of Adam Smith, Freud's *The Interpretation of Dreams*, a few of Jung's treatises, *1984, Darkness at Noon, The Gulag Archipelago, Brave New World,* Shakespeare's best plays, one or two selected religious works, etc. The study of these works would pivot around the **concept of justice.** The initial year of law school would seek to nurture the conscience of prospective jurists. The perceived behavior of lawyers is one of the most powerful sinews connecting the individual citizen to his community.

A few lawyers care more for the documents enumerated above and fair play than anything else. Many lawyers balance their regard for these sacred documents and justice with the need to make a proper living for themselves and their loved ones. Like most people, most lawyers are decent people mainly interested in prospering, while staying within acceptable norms.

Unfortunately, profound avarice and the total lack of a moral compass motivate some of the most superlative corporate barristers and tax attorneys ever to graduate from a prestigious law school. These gentlemen spend all their time devising and passing into legislation **unjust laws** – laws which would have given Adam Smith apoplexy – that protect and foster the astronomical wealth of the most rich and most powerful reptiles on Wall Street.

Since the 19th century, humorists in America such as Mark Twain have characterized politics and Wall Street as the nests of vipers and vultures. There may not be any cure for the various antics of politicians. But there may be some remedy for Wall Street.

If Wall Street could outlaw forever the mechanism of selling short, require payment up-front of about 90% of the market value for stock sales to any individual or entity, and enforce with greater vigor the laws against insider trading, while strengthening that legislation which already exists, many financial crises could be averted. Greedy entrepreneurs, swindlers, and enemy *agents provocateurs* use selling short, very low margins, and insider trading for their own perverse purposes. These faults are a ticking time bomb at the very heart of the American economy. By definition greedy entrepreneurs, swindlers, and enemy *agents provocateurs* are moral cretins.

Adam Smith never discusses the London Stock Market or any of the other stock markets of his time in *Wealth of Nations*. The London Stock Exchange was founded in 1571. Because of the South Sea Bubble which impacted the stock market and other scandals of the early 18th century, Adam Smith and many others felt that the average investor had a better opportunity of calculating his chances of making a profit in an honestly run gambling casino than in the easily manipulated and rigged world of the stock exchange. Smith uses the term stock in various ways in *Wealth of Nations*. Most of the time he is referring to animals on farms or to stationary stock – the machines and materials used in a factory, a warehouse or a retail outfit to create, store, or sell goods. Moveable stock refers to those articles that are for sale to customers. The author does mention private companies offering new issues of stock to individuals who have already invested with them and to the general public through advertisements and by word of mouth. But, to reiterate, he never uses the term 'stock' in a discussion of any stock exchange, nor does he ever bother to explain the workings of any stock exchange.

There are tens of millions of investors in stocks sold on the various stock exchanges in the modern world. Most of these investors carry out their business through financial institutions. A smaller number of people invest on their own. These financial institutions and individuals are largely on the up and up and could not afford to be otherwise.

However, according to some financial experts, the various stock markets are dominated by a handful of people. These individuals are multi-billionaires with incredible power, influence, and access to information not available to the rest of mankind. A small number of this group attempt to carry on their business in the classical tradition of Adam Smith; they are committed to economics with a conscience. But most of this handful pretend they are guided by eco-theological precepts – almost always of the *laissez-faire* variety.

About a third of this handful, in the opinion of many, are also idiot-savants. They can do wondrous things with numbers, like the character so well portrayed by Dustin Hoffman in the film

Rain Man. They spend eighteen hours of each day in front of their computers playing the game of Accumulation – harvesting as much stock market profit as possible – exactly like some teenager addicted to playing a particular pinball machine. Six hours of each day most of them spend sleeping or eating or with loved ones – if they have any. Their enormous earnings they never spend on luxuries, which they do not appreciate, and only the scantest amount of their great wealth on the basic necessities of life. And like the idiot-savant in *Rain Man*, they are incapable of doing some of the simplest things in life, such as speaking properly to a member of the opposite sex or ordering breakfast or filling a car with gas. So amorality in them can be forgiven because they really do not know their asses from their elbows, much less the difference between good and evil. Although they should be forgiven, of course they should not be allowed to wield any power.

If the above estimate is within waving distance of being correct, approximately two thirds of this conspiracy of Moguls who control Wall Street are not idiot-savants. When they spend their excess profits, they buy another mistress or one more yacht or another castle in Spain or one more luxury condo in Paris or diamonds as big as the Ritz, et al. And they do know right from wrong. Yet these people would turn you into a lampshade or lambchop for a single penny or an additional iota of power. Perhaps it is the excess of excellent coke most of them allegedly snort each day in *lieu* of coffee breaks that accounts for their moral turpitude. **What should be your attitude toward such creatures?**

I refer to certain principles put forth in this essay–whose synthesis demonstrates how a modern welfare system should be constructed–as the **Laws of Diminishing Poverty.**

Send all criticisms, comments, and queries to:
frankhsolomon@gmail.com

In order to buy a soft cover copy of this book, go to Amazon.com, type in the following: author's name, Frank Solomon; title, The Manifesto of Capitalism, 13th Edition; and the ISBN # : 978-0-9991384-5-8. To purchase a kindle from Amazon, use:

ISBN#: 978-0-9991384-6-5.

The following song in poetic form is no more corny than the Communist's stirring *Internationale,* the patriotic *Marseillaise* or our own A*merica the Beautiful*. However, music is yet to be found. I am awaiting my Degeyter. —Frank Solomon

Challenge

Arise you creators of the world!
The enemy is before you;
His flag of deprivation is unfurled.

Make ready your arms;
Drive him from the fields;
Your brandished steel alarms
The reeling foe, who yields.
Awaken you master builders,
You architects of freedom,
Weavers of Man's dream,
Minions of light's kingdom.

The throat of poverty is pierced. The host of ignorance recedes.
Arise you creators of the world!
The enemy is before you.
His flag of deprivation is unfurled.

ACKNOWLEDGEMENTS

I wish to thank the following individuals who have helped me over the years in various ways to create the works of which I am the author.

Solomon Jaffe	Alan Pergament Schwartz (Brooksy)
Sondra Solomon	John Voetsch
Meryl A.Volpe	Howard Barnett
Pasquel Rouse	Eleanor Smith
Mrs. Godfrey	Arnold Smith
Marsha Henkin	Francis Volpe
Jerry Henkin	Keith Solomon
Mike Tiesi	Rabbi Johnathan Blake
Evan Podolak	Samuel Rogers
Marvin Adler	Gloria Adler
Esther Adler O'keefe	Mrs. Whalen

Sandro Lomedico

Modern Day Saints

Hugh Hefner
Marilyn Monroe
Albert Einstein
Mikhail Gorbachev
Marlon Brando
Humphrey Bogart
Sigmund Freud
Winston Churchill
Tennessee Williams
Jonas Salk
Elizabeth Taylor
Paul Newman
Charlie Chaplin
Pope Francis
Moshe Dayan
Salvador Dali
Pablo Picasso
James Joyce
George Bernard Shaw
Igor Stravinsky

Modern Day Demons

Hitler
Himmler
Stalin
Mao
Pol Pot
Salazar
Franco
Pablo Escobar
Jeffrey Dahmer
John Wayne Gacy
Ted Bundy
Idi Amin
Dr. Mengele
Eichmann
Goering
Braune
Brack
Gandt
Gebhardt
Goebbels

The Manifesto of Capitalism, 13th Edition tells the truth about Smith's *Wealth of Nations*. The mercantilists are presented as Smith characterized them and as – under other labels – they continue to exist to this day, wrapped in fabrics that disguise their greed, their perfidious nature, and their violence. Fully revealed is the lie that Smith backed *laissez-faire* economics. This volume also includes a detailed presentation of what a 21st century welfare system ought to be about, drawn from Smith's seven page depiction and recommendations for 18th century England. Here is a call for reform that ought to appeal to everyone of good sense who cares about the free enterprise system and his own nation.

A comment from a reader of the *12th Edition of The Manifesto of Capitalism:*

If you read only the preface to this magnificent essay on economics, you will have purchased yourself enough wisdom to last a lifetime. — Pasquel 'Tiger' Rouse, professional boxer and two time world champion kickboxer.

Letters about previous editions of *The Manifesto of Capitalism*:

You ought to teach economic theory in college: you would be a refreshing contrast to those who teach it now.– Hyman Kleinman, Professor Emeritus, Sarah Lawrence College

I found {*The Manifesto of Capitalism*} creative, thoughtful, erudite. It makes us think of great potential for good in our current society in spite of the unfavorable aspects.– Lester D. Friedman, M.D.

Made in the USA
Monee, IL
04 November 2026

67382578R00066